MW01193955

BECOMING CAITLIN CLARK

The Unknown Origin Story of a Modern Basketball Star

Howard Megdal

TRIUMPH
BOOKS

Library of Congress Cataloging-in-Publication Data available upon request.

This book is available in quantity at special discounts for your group or organization. For further information, contact:

Triumph Books LLC
814 North Franklin Street
Chicago, Illinois 60610
(312) 337-0747
www.triumphbooks.com

Printed in U.S.A.
ISBN: 978-1-63727-795-9
Design by Nord Compo

To Mirabelle and Juliet, who make the incredible look routine,
like Caitlin Clark pulling up from the logo.
And to Rachel: life with you is a sellout crowd
at Carver-Hawkeye Arena rising to its feet in collective joy.

Editor's note: this book uses the Associated Press divider between referring to girls *for those high school age and younger and* women *for those college age and older.*

Contents

Foreword

When Howard asked me to write the foreword for his book, *Becoming Caitlin Clark*, it was a no-brainer. First of all, Howard is a wonderful sportswriter who has invested in women's basketball throughout his career and continues to tell the story about our compelling game. He's covered women's basketball on every level and is the perfect person to tell this story. Another reason I wanted to contribute was my love for this game and the state that I spent most of my life in.

Iowa certainly isn't the birthplace of basketball, but it gave it a nudge along the way. We've had basketball in Iowa for more than 100 years. And we may not have always played it the way that you think of—sometimes six on six, sometimes with a rover getting to run the full court. Yeah, we were one of the last to change to the traditional five on five that we all know and love today. Traditions die hard in this state, a state that loved girls basketball, especially in the small communities where towns would shut down on game nights. The stars of those teams became celebrities. Parks and streets were named after them, and parades were held in their honor.

Iowa is also home to the University of Iowa, where Christine Grant spent most of her professional career as our director of women's athletics and worked tirelessly to promote gender equity in women's sport. And yes, of course, Iowa is also home to Caitlin Clark, the phenom who helped women's basketball reach record extraordinary heights. I first saw Caitlin play in seventh grade and I knew that this kid had something special. She had moxie, she had confidence, she had game. And I was blessed to coach her. Caitlin came around at the right time. People were beginning to take notice of the great game of women's basketball and they seized upon this star. She had the skills and the personality to bring our game to the forefront, to record-breaking crowds both in person and on television. Everywhere she went people wanted to see this kid who could make logo threes or pass on a dime.

Caitlin is a star, but she also understands she stands on the shoulders of the women that were stars before her. And much of that foundation was planted right here in this state, where, yes, corn grows, but so do young women athletes.

—Lisa Bluder, Iowa head coach, 2000–2024

Introduction

When it was over—the final moments of Caitlin Clark's 2024 WNBA season that was the most impactful rookie campaign anyone could ever remember in ways both measurable by the present and exciting for the future—Caitlin Clark left the Indiana Fever's visiting locker room at Mohegan Sun Arena, where Indiana had just been eliminated from the WNBA playoffs by Alyssa Thomas and the home team, and walked confidently through the industrial white brick corridor leading to the postgame press conference with assembled media.

Clark sat at a podium, as she had so many times before, and reflected on all she had done. She did so not in a dedicated media room. The WNBA, unlike its older, more established brother league, the NBA, often plays in arenas without that accoutrement, one of the many ways the league—and really women's basketball itself—has been forced to adapt in real time during Caitlin Clark's rise.

The game itself, of course, was a sellout—customary and expected now. She'd maxed out the 8,910-seat Mohegan Sun Arena each of the four times she played there. She'd sold out all but four of her home dates back in Indiana at Bankers

Life Fieldhouse, and each of those four games fell just shy of a sellout while exceeding 15,000 fans. To put that in perspective, her smallest crowd of the 2024 season, May 30 against the Seattle Storm, drew 15,022 fans. That was also larger than any crowd who went to see the Fever prior to Clark's arrival since September 18, 2016, when all-time great Tamika Catchings played in her final regular-season game for Indiana with playoff seeding on the line.

So much time, energy, and angst in 2024 revolved around debating precisely why Clark reverberated within American culture, elevating the sport of women's basketball like nothing that had come before her. Easy, simple answers focused on elements of her singularity. Resentment from many, who have spent lifetimes working to build the sport, only to be cut out of a present-centric view of it also spilled into view. But these poles do not represent how the overwhelming majority of figures—both trailblazers and the current and future stars who will lead us into the next generations—within the game experienced the past and present or view what's ahead. There is a symbiotic relationship within necessary building that took place over the previous century, creating the conditions for Clark's supernova emergence onto the world stage.

And just as important: Clark herself, while a product of these efforts found everywhere but so often born in Iowa, rose to the challenge of taking the baton just as women's basketball's perfect storm formed around her career. There is no Caitlin Clark without women pioneers playing basketball as soon as the game itself was created by James A. Naismith in the 1890s.

There is no Caitlin Clark without Iowa. Unlike many other states early in the 20th century, Iowa moved to protect the game itself for women from those who would destroy opportunities for women in the name of protecting them. There is no Caitlin Clark without a generation of Iowa girls playing the game in the first two decades of the 20th century, excelling while reveling in the support of their communities. There is no Caitlin Clark without the Iowa Girls High School Athletic Union making the brave decision to protect varsity basketball. Just as significant, there is no Caitlin Clark without that game's rules themselves—the six-on-six game, which has come to shape the modern offense and prizes the skills that separate Clark from even the greatest who came before her, not to mention the critical voices who molded her into the player she is.

There is no Caitlin Clark without the 1962 Van Horne Hornettes, who redefined success on the court, paving the way for a faster-paced, perimeter-oriented game. There is no Caitlin Clark without Van Horne itself, who paved the way on how to properly fete a women's basketball breakthrough.

There is no Caitlin Clark without Molly Bolin, whose rise came through the Iowa girls system, which left no small-town star without a chance to prove her greatness and whose star power was limitless as her shooting range. But her efforts came with both incredible professional and personal costs. There is no Caitlin Clark without Lark Birdsong planting a stake in the ground for the University of Iowa's women's basketball program and Christine Grant funding it at a level equal to other women's sports—itself a battleground.

There is no Caitlin Clark without C. Vivian Stringer, whose vision of a sold-out Carver-Hawkeye Arena to support an Iowa team filled with stars from around the country created the very canvas Clark drew on, or Jolette Law, who was imported from South Carolina to run Stringer's team as its point guard and engine before shaping the roster of Dawn Staley's Gamecocks, one of the endless Iowa diaspora defining the women's game today.

There is no Caitlin Clark without the visionary basketball minds and supporters of women Lisa Bluder and Jan Jensen, the products of the six-on-six game, taking the twin pillars of elite post play and perimeter magic and molding an offense-first attack that draws eyeballs in the millions, the excitement as overwhelming as when the game itself thrilled packed gymnasiums all over small towns in Iowa. Jensen's grandmother, Dorcas Andersen, helped create that excitement over a century ago just as Jensen built on what Clark herself created as the leader of the Hawkeyes program.

None of what Clark, a preternatural talent at not only the game of basketball itself, but also at serving as a public avatar for the hopes, dreams, love, and hate of a passionate group of fans living through tumultuous American times—all as she only recently exited her teenage years—would be possible without Clark herself. And none of it happens without the elements of every single predecessor you'll meet in this book, on and off the court, for more than a century preceding Clark's arrival on the scene.

Every single one of these trailblazers, including Clark herself, have one thing in common.

For all their disparate ways, they altered the course of women's basketball for—and often with—one another. Their love of the game is only fully understood within the larger context of what it means to engage in the work, the joy, the devastation of loss, and elation of victories large and small with the people they love. It is the given for boys and men, always has been. Turning women's basketball into that given—for the fully realized life that comes with such progress—is what resonates most deeply with Clark, with all who helped produce her, and with the countless girls and women who will benefit from her ascension.

That is what was on Clark's mind, what was found inscribed on her heart when she was asked what her first professional season meant to her on the night it came to an end, while workers noisily prepared the arena for another event, and gamblers by the hundreds pulled on slot machines and pushed their chips forward in the casino overhead.

What mattered most to the woman at the center of a movement that so many had worked for and so many others had breathlessly predicted would never arrive? "I feel like there's been so many amazing moments, but it's the moments that none of you see that I enjoy the most," Clark said, and she visibly relaxed as she said it. "It's not the basketball. It's the people that I get to spend it with. Whether it's my family, whether it's my teammates, that's what's been most special for myself. And I feel like those people are the people that know me best. Those are the people that I really care about. So at the end of the day, basketball is basketball. I think it is what it is, and the people around me are what allow me to be really good at it, allow me to have a lot of fun, allow me to be myself...there's been a lot of great moments, making the playoffs, getting drafted, making the national championship game. That's all really cool, but at the end of the day, it's the people and the relationships and the memories outside of that, and if it's not that for you as a professional athlete, I feel like you're doing it wrong."

Clark's view of why women's basketball matters was echoed by so many I spoke with for this book. The chance to play the game of basketball to the level and limit of their talent is a path that is still sought by women throughout the country for all the gains we've seen, but the earliest and fullest manifestations of it came in Iowa and set a pattern for women's basketball we are now seeing replicated at a worldwide scale. Playing basketball and being fully celebrated for it opens the world for women in ways that extend into every corner of professional life.

So it was for Lillian Paula (Haeussler) Randall, a remarkable renaissance woman who spent decades as a biochemist in California before her second career as a sculptor landed her in *Who's Who in American Art*. She also—and not incidentally—starred decades earlier as the center for the Alden High School girls basketball team located in Alden, Iowa, just outside of Iowa Falls. That's not to say earning the support of her family to join the team was easy. To even attend high school, Randall needed to earn money to help support her family, which she did one cent at a time while taking portraits with her Brownie camera—first of friends, then of other residents as her reputation grew—and developing them herself using the instructions she found in a Sears, Roebuck and Co. catalog.

The town of Alden had a population of 699, according to the 1910 U.S. Census. "[It had] a high percentage of college-trained citizens who cheered us in our one girl's athletic pursuit: basketball," Randall recalled.

Sixty years later she met up with her high school coach, Martha Granzow Roberson. By then, in 1974, Randall was 78 and Roberson was 84. But the two spoke on their annual visit "of the togetherness basketball brought with it, how the practice sessions as well as the games built us up physically and psychologically," Randall said. "We had never heard of penetrating [the lane against] our opponents, of getting credit for rebounds, or containing a threatening basket shooter. We just played—as hard as we could—and loved every minute of it."

None of it came easily. But basketball called to Randall the way it has to so many women throughout the history of the game. The constant is the lure of the sport. The variable is the opportunities to play it, how often, and at what level. "As soon as I felt at ease in my new environment, I became keenly aware of something I had never known of before: basketball for girls!" Randall said. "Not only did I need to make time for my family chores, for Latin studies, algebra, etc., somehow, some way, I had to try out for basketball."

She devised a scheme to overcome the objections of her father, a minister who objected to women undertaking any endeavor in bloomers, which he considered "men's attire." By trying out, making the team, and winning the first game all in secret, she believed she could engender sufficient "parental pride to nullify all objections." Randall was correct. Soon after, the 1914 Alden High School girls basketball team—with uniforms each girl made herself out of seven-and-a-half yards of wide black serge, the school having only enough funding for the team's basketball, games being played on muddy dirt courts, and players with their hair tied up with red bandanas—won the Hardin County championship.

Yet all those years later, thinking back to the pursuit that set her on a course of success in science and art alike, this is what Randall remembered most fondly about her basketball years.

"We had team outings, which I have never forgotten. In winter there were sleigh rides, the steaming breath of horses puffing clouds along the way. Their manes were often frosty, and icicles grew on their ring bits. We thrilled to the rhythmic jingle of sleigh bells and sang mostly Stephen Foster songs as we nestled in the protective straw," she said. "We tumbled out, usually at the home of some team member who lived on a farm. There we found a great isinglass stove red hot with hard coal burning and the cook stove ready with coffee and cakes. In the meantime we toasted marshmallows and hot dogs over an open fire and sang and shouted for the sheer joy of youth."

Not a game-winning basket, nor holding a trophy aloft—that is not what connected Randall to the game. And 110 years later, Clark, possessor of many gifts, though not the benefit of age as she considered a similar question to the one Randall answered late in her life, understood this at the age of 22 even in the aftermath of the ultimate competitor's loss, which ended her rookie season. "Championships are great, and hopefully we have a few of those," Clark said, the small smile an implicit promise that in her mind there's no "hopefully" about it. "But you want to have really good relationships with people at the end of the day. So [I] feel like it's all of that, and you can't put your finger on just one thing because there's so many."

Here's the story of how Lillian, Dorcas, Molly, Vivian, Jolette, Lisa, and Jan all built the opportunity for Caitlin to wrap her arms around the life that she is fully embracing and just what it means for everyone who comes next. And when Clark met the moment, she maximized it fully.

CHAPTER ONE

Dorcas and an Institution

As long as Americans have played basketball, women have played basketball. And nowhere did the passion for the game take root as completely in ways that opened the pipeline for generations who followed the early adopters of the game to grow it into the internationally popular and financially lucrative business of today than in Iowa.

In the winter of 1891, James A. Naismith invented the game of basketball. By 1892 Senda Berenson was teaching young women to play the game at Smith College in Northampton, Massachusetts. The game quickly spread from those who learned it in the northeast, and by 1893 women began to play the game in Iowa at the Dubuque YMCA. By 1894 women at Iowa Agricultural College (later Iowa State) and University of Iowa began playing at their local YMCAs, while Grinnell College incorporated it into its physical education curriculum. By 1898 an intramural game was scheduled, played before fans, and even covered in the *Dubuque High Echo* student paper.

Of course, the game looked very different. The ball itself wasn't standardized. Frequently oblong, the leather concoction was hardly built for dribbling. The courts were not courts at all. Surfaces, usually outdoors, consisted of grass or dirt. One early game between Elma and Alta Vista High School on July 4, 1904, took place on a grass field that had been burned off for the occasion, and the players' bloomers were covered in soot by the end of the game.

Seasons often lingered as late into the fall as weather would allow. Due to the late sunsets, the summer served as the best time of year to play. This beat the indoor alternatives usually available at that time, as Janice A. Beran wrote in her 1993 book about Iowa women's basketball: "Games were also played in community opera houses, church basements, and schools, above stores, and once in awhile above a saloon. Each place had its own challenges for the players. Some were small; some had life-threatening obstacles. The indoor places were usually heated by a wood-burning stove that was located more often than not smack-dab in the center of the floor."

Despite the stoves—usually lit hours before by the boys' team—and the bloomer-based uniforms featuring heavy, long-sleeved blouses and black stockings underneath the ankle-length bloomers, a frequent complaint came from how cold it was for the players. Still, those schools who could find indoor or outdoor places to play that could also seat spectators experienced something consistently. From virtually the beginning of the sport, not only did girls and women in Iowa find that they loved to play the game of basketball, but also girls and boys, men and women alike took joy in watching them play as well.

Iowa is not some outlier when it comes to how quickly and how intensely girls and women fell in love with the game of basketball. Out in California, for instance, Stanford played Cal at San Francisco's Page Street Armory on April 4, 1896. Although only women were allowed in the official attendance of 700 strong, another group of men observed from the windows around the armory's ceiling. What followed, of course, was a slow strangling of the future Pac-12 and now ACC rivalry. First, Stanford banned all women's intercollegiate athletics in 1899 in order to protect the students, of course, while avoiding, according to *The Stanford Daily*, "the unpleasant publicity accompanying the contests," a better window into the true motives of the move. Cal had not only a team, but also a gym of its own, Hearst Hall, built by William Randolph Hearst's mother, Patricia A. "Phoebe" Hearst. But with other schools around the state moving in a similar direction as Stanford in banning women's sports, the team ultimately disbanded in 1907, the year the men's team was designated as the college's varsity basketball team. Prioritizing men's basketball over women's basketball wasn't an inevitability forced by interest or participation. It was a series of conscious choices, a gender construct.

Let's take Illinois, for example. As historian Scott Johnson chronicled: "Not long after the introduction of basketball as an athletic activity for high school girls, all levels of the educational hierarchy were engaged in a debate over its merits. As a simple playground game, girls basketball had prompted few objections. However, when girls started developing interscholastic programs that rivaled those of the boys, basketball quickly turned into a nightmare for school administrators. While students and sympathetic teachers pushed for more interschool play, school principals and professional educators marshaled their resistance to what they perceived as the masculinization of the female athletic program.

"This scenario played itself out in practically every state during the early 20th century but perhaps nowhere so early as in Illinois. The girls basketball revolution started in Illinois in 1895 and within a dozen years developed into a statewide network that included teams at up to 300 high schools. In basketball at least, high school girls became the athletic equals of boys—forming teams and leagues, scheduling games and transportation, issuing challenges and upholding school pride. Girls teams received broad support from the student body, both male and female, and uniformly positive reviews from the popular press. Perhaps because girls athletics was new and exciting, many of these teams received public attention that outstripped their male counterparts.

"Not surprisingly, many school administrators saw dubious value in young ladies acting like young men. They were joined in their fight against girls interscholastics by many female physical educators who believed in the importance of athletics for girls but not when it meant duplicating the objectionable aspects of the male athletic model. The opposing forces gathered steam slowly, but eventually they were able to install a ban on all interscholastic competition among high school girls. The first incarnation of girls interscholastic basketball in Illinois was dead in 1907."

By 1900, 300 women played in an intramural league, including players from Northwestern University and University of Chicago at the same time both schools struggled to find enough men to form even a single men's team. And yet the appeal to play varsity games between the two schools—with each team earning a letter—was denied by both schools' faculties.

Meanwhile, in Iowa not only were collegiate teams like Iowa State thriving with rosters north of 20 women, but they'd also often play against men, as when they faced the Iowa State men's team on the grass in the center of campus in 1903. Losing just 19–17, the student paper declared at the end of its story on the game: "The girls deserve much praise for the way in which they developed in such a short time…we hope basketball and athletics for girls will be a permanent thing."

To be clear: retrograde factions have always worked to slow the game down, or eliminate it entirely, in Iowa, too. But these voices were drowned out again and again at critical moments that kept Iowa girls and women playing. As a result, the stability of girls and women's basketball played out very differently in Iowa than anywhere else in the country. Critical actions by small groups of people who realized what the sport could mean to everyone set off a chain reaction that helped create the conditions for the rise of Caitlin Clark a century later.

It is important to remember that the value and danger of interscholastic sports themselves were a matter of public debate in the first decade of the 20th century. Indeed, the number of deaths in football alone led to the sport's reform becoming a key, multi-decade crusade of Teddy Roosevelt, including a summit at the White House. Of course, Roosevelt often argued for the value of football in retrograde, gender-defining ways, telling an audience in 1903 that he believed "in rough games and rough, manly sports" while urging reformers in 1906 not to "emasculate football" or to play it "on too ladylike a basis."

Meanwhile, the concerns as they related to women were very different. In Illinois much of the early growth in women's basketball took place in and around the city of Chicago in Cook County. This made a wholesale ban easier to conceive of and enforce. The rise of thought leaders of the time provided a scaffolding of intellectual argument more than sufficient for overwhelmingly male scholastic bureaucrats to force it through. For instance, Francis Kellor, an educator who had witnessed the rise of Cook County interscholastic girls basketball in the first few years of the 1900s, said this at a physical education conference in 1906: "The principles underlying [women's sports] must differ from those which are carried out in men's sports today. These essential principles are: 1) Sports must be conducted for the good of the number and not for the purpose of getting good material for championship teams. 2) The predominating note in women's sports should always be the joy and exhilaration and fun of playing, not the grim determination to win at any cost. 3) Women's games are for themselves and for their school or college. With few exceptions, the standards of women's athletic contests do not possess sufficient educational value to justify giving them before indiscriminate audiences who pay admission fees."

Fellow educator Elma L. Warner cited the lack of interest in the girls game by the faculty, the lack of trained coaches, and the potential for players to experience "faintness, hysteria, or melancholy" as reasons to—rather than hire faculty interested in promoting the game and training coaches, who were being found all over the country to modernize the men's game, to do the same for the women's game—simply disband women's interscholastic basketball altogether.

These two essays, both published in the *American Physical Education Review* in 1906, helped turn the tide in Cook County, which saw its league reduced from 11 teams to five before disbanding altogether a year later.

But Iowa's school system was more advanced in the rural areas of the state and well-established within them. A number of midwestern states mandated the creation of local schools, which needed to stay open for the vast majority of the year and collect taxes to support them. The resulting growth, particularly in Iowa, saw a drop in illiteracy rates to the lowest levels across the country, while Iowa itself led the nation in number of schoolhouses, with more than 14,000 by 1900. The identity of the small towns across the state had been inextricably linked to their schools. And by far the most popular game for girls in Iowa, as the 20th century dawned, was basketball.

So as the state of Iowa began its losing battle against the efforts from Progressive Era reformers to consolidate its school system—to be fair, one in which Iowa held out for most of the 20th century—the pride in its girls basketball teams was baked into that life and tradition. As Max McIlwain wrote in *The Only Dance in Iowa*, "Country schools already brought community residents together because they were almost always the only communal property a rural township held."

And what they did when they gathered much of the time was to cheer on their girls basketball teams. In Boone, Iowa, with a population of 8,880 in 1900, the presence of an indoor gym allowed the high school to charge admission when the senior class played the sophomores. The following year boys were allowed to watch, and attendance swelled while all four classes fielded teams in the Boone High School Athletic Association. By the end of the decade, Boone High School teams played at Iowa State against the early versions of the Cyclones.

No matter how small the town, girls basketball took hold across the state. The population of Elma, Iowa, was only 976 in 1900, and the town itself only had been incorporated in the late 1880s with the post office built in 1886. Fifteen years later a young woman named Harriet Williams was drawn to a game brought home from Missouri by her older sister in which round balls were thrown into peach baskets. By 1904 Williams became the ambassador for the game in her town as she recalled in a 1989 interview with

Beran: "I was the only one who knew anything about it. At 14 I was quite tall. They set up some basketballs on a grassy plot. We didn't dribble. We just passed. We shot with a chest push pass and with a one hand underhand shot. There were many people who came to watch us. They stood several rows deep, watching us play on the school ground. Some of the mothers thought it was terrible, but my mother and some other parents encouraged it."

As a result of this widespread acceptance and acclaim for playing—incidentally, one of the other factors Warner had cited in her 1906 polemic against girls basketball receiving too much media attention—multiple generations of Iowa girls grew up with playing basketball as a pinnacle of joy and achievement among extracurricular activities.

Into this world of burgeoning opportunity, Dorcas Marie Elizabeth Andersen was born to Jens C. and Marie Karen Jensen Andersen on September 29, 1902, on their farm in Sharon Township, which borders both Kimballton and Audubon. The nearest incorporated town, Kimballton, was not listed in the 1900 census, and by 1910 it checked in with 271 people, including an eight-year-old Dorcas. For Dorcas life revolved around family and her hometown, Audubon. She was baptized and ultimately confirmed at Our Savior's Lutheran Church right in town and attended school in town up through Audubon High School. She arrived there in

1917, and by then a generation of girls had discovered the joy of playing basketball. Andersen earned the nickname "Lottie"—for the lot of points she scored—and helped lead her team to the semifinals of the first-ever state tournament held at Drake University in her junior season in 1920 and to victory in her senior season in 1921.

The team created a following that not only included raucous home crowds, but also on the road as well despite often-difficult travel conditions. "The Exira boys won 38–6, and the Audubon girls won 22–18 in a doubleheader basketball game played here last evening by the high school teams of the two towns," a reporter wrote in the *Atlantic News Telegraph* on January 21, 1920. "There was a big crowd in attendance, many fans accompanying the Audubon players." Now, that trip is a quick jaunt down Route 71, but that road didn't open until 1926. Audubon's fans were undaunted.

By March of 1920, Andersen, coached by the legendary superintendent M.M. McIntire, prepared to go to the state tournament at Drake University in Des Moines for the first-ever tournament held in a statewise, organized fashion. Previously, various teams who had won their county titles would declare themselves state champs. This would decide it definitively. "I got a new hat for $7.25," Andersen wrote in a diary entry labeled March 15, 1920, according to Andersen's granddaughter, University of Iowa head coach Jan Jensen, though Andersen played through the end of the 1921 season. "I also got several other things [because] I'm getting ready for the Des Moines basketball tournament. This eve I went to basketball practice, and after practice I could have just cried as it was my last basketball practice in the Audubon gym for me as I graduate this spring. It was just like saying goodbye to a very dear friend at practice this eve. Superintendent McIntyre sent me to the doctor, as I've been having a bad cough for some time, and he wanted me to be rid of it before I went to the tournament. As he said, he wanted me to be in first-class condition."

Whichever tournament she'd been preparing for at that moment, she found herself among Iowa girls basketball's best in the March of her junior season. That very first Iowa state tournament included Audubon and champion Correctionville, who knocked off Audubon in the semifinals and captured the championship by defeating Nevada 11–4. The teams split the profits; each school earned $2.43.

But in her senior season, Andersen would not be denied. Proving her nickname was apropos, she scored 89 of Audubon's 122 points in six games played over two days, culminating in a 21–11 victory against Ottumwa. "The victors played two games on the first day and four on the second," a reporter wrote in the *Atlantic News Telegraph* on March 21, 1921, "one more than its opponents, who, despite the one game advantage of rest, could not stop the accuracy of Dorcas Anderson [sic], star forward who made eight field goals." (Let the record show the misspelling of her name annoys Jan Jensen. "Don't be messing up that Danish sen," she mock-cautioned.)

"Miss Anderson displayed a wonderful accurate eye for baskets," the *Atlantic News Telegraph* continued. "Her playing was not of the sensational order. She possessed sufficient reach to enable her to keep the ball well above the opposing guards."

Worth noting here is that Andersen played center, a place where many of the dominant six-on-six players excelled for much of Iowa basketball history. In this way she parallels the rise of Jensen herself six decades later but not the exquisite passing and long-range bombs from Clark. This is the birth of Iowa as a cradle of basketball stardom; the innovations that produced Clark the player would come later.

Undaunted by the dissenting review by the reporter, Audubon's boys celebrated their fellow star athlete as their own hero. "Ten of the strongest Audubon boys lifted and hoisted me up in the air and carried me around the gym," Andersen recalled. "They did it to honor me, but I didn't appreciate it that way."

As forward-thinking as Andersen was—and her life would prove that again and again—she still, as the first champion to be celebrated this way, struggled to reconcile it, pushing into the headwinds of how women were expected to conduct themselves. A young woman in Iowa experienced opportunities and goals differently in basketball, but Iowa was still on planet Earth. Still in America. The push and pull even among true advocates for women's athletics about how much to celebrate the women who reach the top of the sport has never really stopped. Not even with Clark.

Andersen felt so many emotions at this moment of triumph. Yes, she was proud of the game she played, thankful to God, and delighted to share in the moment with so many of her friends and family. But inescapably, as the tournament prepared to present her with a silver loving cup—one she vowed in her diary that "I will prize and honor mine as long as I live"—her thoughts turned to this end point: that there would be no more basketball for her after this remarkable run through the best players and teams the state could throw at her.

Incidentally, she did keep and treasure the trophy. The cup now resides in the office of Jensen, the P. Sue Beckwith-endowed head basketball coach at Iowa. (Beckwith was yet another high-achieving Iowa girls basketball player. She starred for Boone High School before the Hawkeyes, then embarked on a successful medical career.). Rereading her grandmother's words over a century later, Jensen understood the disparate emotions Andersen felt at this high-water moment of her basketball career. When she read those words from her grandmother in the diaries Jensen discovered during the COVID-19 pandemic, she was transported not only to the end of Andersen's career, but also to her own. "She wrote, 'I'm sad because I feel like I've lost a good friend,'" Jensen read aloud. "And I think that's anybody in sport or when you end a season. That's what it feels like because you're devoting so much time…. That's your identity, that's your passion. And when it ends, there is kind of that mourning, right?"

Andersen, like many of her fellow competitors in the state tournament, followed a particular path. She attended Iowa State Teachers' College, got her degree, came home to teach in tiny schools with names like Lone Willow Douglas No. 6, Pleasant View Douglas No. 2, The Viola Consolidated School, Rose Hill No. 8, and Old Hamlin No. 1. She taught her young students something else, too: basketball.

When she got married in 1928, though, to Donald D. Randolph right in the same Audubon church where she'd been baptized, all that had to end. As Melba Gardemann Olsen, star of the 1927 state championship team—her steal in the waning moments preserved a 38–37 win against Sioux Center—recalled in her oral history: "I was fortunate to have the opportunity to move to Conrad, teaching second grade, coaching girls high school basketball and girls high school physical education (a new requirement).… There was always a clause in my teaching contract, 'should Miss Gardemann marry, the contract would be void.' In 1934 winter came with much snowfall in December. Merle Olson and his dad had gone by horses and bobsled to get groceries at Newhall. On the return trip from Newhall, my brother, Merle Gardemann, visited with the Olsons and asked Merle Olson to stop off at the farm. I'm sure my brother had intentions to help 'cupid,' for he informed Merle Olson that his sister was in the house. I believe that my brother thought his sister and his neighbor, both 25, should be more than casual friends. He was right, and that was the beginning of a relationship that lasted for over 59 years since that cold December day in 1934.

"We corresponded almost daily (3 cents postage on letters). Because I had a possible contract to teach second grade and coach girls high school basketball for 1936–37, we decided to keep our marriage on May 9, 1936 a secret. We didn't even tell my brother. Merle's two sisters, Gertrude and Ariel, were our witnesses. In those years because of the scarcity of jobs, married lady teachers were not permitted to teach. We started for Geneseo, Illinois, at about 5:30 AM in my 1930 Model A. When we arrived in Geneseo, we learned that it was not the county seat! We hurried to Cambridge before the courthouse closed at noon and secured the marriage license. Our next stop was at the parsonage of Reverend A. S. Hamilton, who was a fellow Lutheran. After 'fortifying' himself with what smelled like grape wine, he pronounced us man and wife. Our wedding picture was taken by Ariel with a box camera. We were posed in front of a statue on the courthouse lawn…. Our secret marriage was not a secret very long. A young lady from Newhall, employed in Davenport, read the news in a city newspaper. We rented a house in Van Horne for $12 a month on July 1st. After returning to Conrad to finish my year, I called a faculty meeting early one morning and served 'newlyweds' an ice cream sandwich. This completed our secret wedding."

It also ended Olsen's coaching career. Practically, what this meant was that while across the country this discrimination against married women lasted into the early 1960s, in Iowa specifically, one of the few places where women were growing up playing basketball in large numbers, an overwhelming majority of those women were not permitted to take on coaching jobs for an extended period of time. The ancillary impact of that on how many of Iowa's best basketball minds were indirectly banned from the game—and the shape of who was permitted to coach—continued to be felt deep into the 21st century. So while tremendous barriers remained to be scaled by the women's game, the basic building blocks of love and respect for it—among the players themselves with universal appeal across the sexes—already began a foundation for what Clark would accomplish a century later. "I mean, look at that," Jansen marveled, considering the scene her grandmother had described of getting paraded around a gym and that a girls basketball champion was celebrated by boys. "Think of the significance of that. No one was saying, 'Dorcas, go get me a sandwich.' They were coming and putting her on their shoulders and only, only down when [she's saying], 'Come on, please put me down. This is embarrassing.'"

Andersen's basketball career ended that night on the floor of the Drake University Fieldhouse, but her impact on the world was just beginning. She spent 54 years as president of the Audubon County Republican Committee, though Jensen pointed out her politics were more of a proto-Nancy Pelosi than the modern-day Republicans. She collected countless bylines as a reporter for local newspapers, often syndicating her own work, an Iowa Associated Press unto herself. Her faith strengthened her family bonds and her community engagement alike. And her influence on both the decision-makers who would help define the sport, both immediately after her career ended right through the present day, is undeniable.

That influence began with her alma mater, Audubon High School, itself. She brought home a championship in 1921 before graduating, leading the all-state first team honors. And that foundation of excellence continued at Audubon, where M.M. McIntire, who oversaw the program while serving as superintendent of schools in the district, would pilot the team to four straight state titles as part of Iowa's first dynasty. McIntire would serve several vital functions in the history of Iowa women's basketball. He kept a close, watchful eye on his players and the Audubon program, helping to define what would be possible for a successful high school girls program. Andersen remembered McIntire instructing her boyfriend that he had only one rule for the two of them—on the night before a game, she must be home by 10:00 PM. The way small towns worked allowed McIntire to also send his son to, as she remembered, "'Watch what Dorcas orders when you go out to eat' to be sure I ate right."

Although in hindsight this sounds overly paternalistic to many, it reflects just how seriously McIntire took girls basketball as an institution even in these early days of the sport at a moment when the debate raged about whether the sport should even exist at all. Figures in education massed within two primary arguments against competitive girls high school basketball. Some believed that it would be detrimental to the health of women to play at a high level. Others worried the focus on select, talented players in a sport would preclude general physical education for all girls and women. The idea voiced commonly as "a sport for every girl and every girl in a sport" argued for equality without the ability to advance. That such a model differed from the way boys were encouraged to compete was considered a feature, not a bug by many educators of the time—even from some physicians who believed in the pseudoscience of the dangers of the sport. (Here again Beran's research is vital. Comprehensive data shows that an overwhelming majority of the women who played basketball during this time were actually happier, stronger, and more socially well-adjusted than their non-basketball peers.)

An additional reason, usually unstated, was that at the bigger schools, a crush of teams for boys made gym time a hot commodity, and the easiest answer for many was to simply sideline girls to help ease the traffic. But in small school districts all over Iowa, a state built on a generation of pride and glory brought by girls basketball, more than sufficient room was made for both the girls and boys to play any sport they wished. There was one gym but less enrollment, and the enthusiasm for girls basketball far outpaced any concerns about whether everyone would get a chance to play or the inherent dangers of celebrating those who excelled too much.

Even so, 284 members of the Iowa High School Athletic Association (IHSAA) crowded into the Central Presbyterian Church, then located at the corner of Eighth and High Street in Des Moines, and overwhelmingly voted to join the movement all over the country to ban girls basketball. McIntire even floated a compromise measure that would allow for individual districts to decide on their own, but that wasn't even put to a vote by the IHSAA, which seemed eager to exercise control over the process. When the final tally was recorded, 259 members of the IHSAA attempted to end girls basketball in Iowa. But 25 members did not. McIntire did not. John W. Agans of Mystic High School did not, instead telling his fellow administrators just what a mistake they'd be making: "Gentlemen, if you attempt to do away with girls basketball in Iowa, you'll be standing at the center of the track when the train runs over you!"

The Associated Press reported on these events the next day. "An attack on girls basketball in the schools of the state as a menace to motherhood and maidenly modesty featured the meeting of the state athletic association," a quite-possibly tongue-in-cheek report described the events on November 7, 1925. "After 90 minutes of debate, a resolution designed to force the state board of control to banish the girls sport from Iowa high schools was adopted." The astute reporter then added: "Interviews with prominent members of the athletic association, however, failed to bring promise of the immediate effectiveness of the resolution." This is the first mention, if only by implication, of the Iowa Girls High School Athletic Union (IGHSAU).

Agans, McIntire, and the other breakaway administrators decided if the IHSAA wouldn't sponsor girls basketball tournaments, they'd do it themselves. Incidentally, there is a considerable amount of contemporary reporting suggesting that the backlash from the IHSAA's decision manifested itself immediately. By December of 1925, it was explained in *The Des Moines Register* sports pages that "no attempt to prohibit girls from playing has been made," according to a statement provided by the IHSAA that sounds like a classic attempt at public relations cleanup. The statement went on to note that if another group wished to organize tournaments for girls basketball, it was welcome to do so—a far cry from the tone of the November meeting.

Already, the IGHSAU had begun to change history. As a contemporary superintendent, G.L. Sanders, said, reflecting on the moment in 1948: "These men all did jobs for which their names will go down in history—from all who believe in girls basketball and from the girls who play. Their sincerity and integrity were beyond question; anything they did was for the best interest of the girls."

The response was extraordinary—159 schools signed up for the IGHSAU tournament structure of county, then sectional, qualifiers for the state tournament. By 1927 simply meeting Agans was notable enough for Melba Gardemann Olson to mention it in her oral history 66 years later in

1993. Agans also coached the Mystic High team, which reached the semifinals of the 1927 tournament, the second one under the auspices of the IGHSAU. Olson's Newhall team would win it all in her senior season. A few months later, she graduated with a class of 16 people, and then it was on to Iowa State Teachers' College—now called the University of Northern Iowa—where basketball was still of the intramural variety. Big-time varsity women's college basketball, even in Iowa, was many decades away.

With survival now assured, girls basketball in Iowa entered growth and development mode. A rule that divided the court into thirds with six players to a side and the court divided into halves was liberalized in 1934. Suddenly, a modern, up-tempo feel accompanied all the loyalty and intensity of the game. Bloomers gave way to shorts and tops, which allowed girls to play and shoot more freely. Membership in the IGHSAU grew steadily—up 7 percent in 1937 at which point the IGHSAU refunded members their $3 fee due to the organization operating in the black for the first time. They repeated that in 1938, as membership rose another 12 percent. Over a decade the tournament saw revenue increase from less than $2,000 to north of $15,000 a year—and did that during a slight economic hiccup called the Great Depression. Morry Shadle, sports editor of *The* (Council

Bluffs) *Daily Nonpareil*, said that "Boys basketball is the No. 2 sport in many southwest Iowa localities."

Even a figure as well-versed in the growth of the game as the younger McIntire still warned in an interview with Shadle that the game should not grow too big. "If we permit more promotions through the sponsorship of girls basketball, we are going to lose because too much play will coarsen girls," he said. But the growth continued to quicken without any subsequent complaints, loss of revenue, or evident coarsening.

By the 1940s the invention of the perfectly spherical ball with no more large seams and capable of being inflated with an air pump helped regulate dribbling. The jump shot was introduced in the late 1930s, and players began shooting with both hands regularly by the end of the following decade.

The gap between Iowa's girls basketball experience and other states was summarized this way by R.H. Chisholm in the 1945 *Iowa Girls Basketball Scrapbook*: "Few girls enjoying the game in Iowa high schools realize the limitations placed on basketball in most other states. In 1945 the National Federation of State High School Athletic Associations, which manages boys' athletics in 39 states, has discouraged girls interscholastic basketball, that is, between different schools, and does not sponsor such a program as the Iowa Girls Union does. For example, Illinois goes no further than to promote a series of telegraphic tournaments for the girls in which they compete against 'certain standards.' Wouldn't this be fun for you Iowa girls who are accustomed to playing in your county, sectional, district, and state tournaments under real-life conditions before large and interested crowds rather than in the seclusion of your gym with your 'coach' sending in a telegraphic report of what you did? Can you imagine what fun a Van Houton, a Moore, a Coomes, a Schuneman, or an Armstrong would have from this type of competition? And can you think of what interest you might have in this type of play? In the states of Georgia, Maryland, Missouri, Iowa, South Carolina, and Tennessee, interschool contests, and tournaments are held, but in the other states the activity is either frowned upon or openly forbidden."

Daughters of stars began to take their place in Iowa stardom, and Iowa newspapers turned players into celebrities. By 1947 70 percent of all high school girls in Iowa played basketball. Of course, this all took place on planet Earth and in America, so even in Iowa, Gene Shumate needed to make the following point to Red Barber on his 1947 CBS Sports report about the Iowa women's basketball phenomenon: "The states, which do not permit girls high school basketball, do so on the grounds that the competition would spoil a girls' sense of femininity. We can't agree with that in Iowa. We've taken to our hearts these lassies who play all out and race madly hither and yon but still remember to pause in the midst of a scoring rally to adjust a hair ribbon. We think it's the greatest show on Earth."

And guess who else was watching the high school girls? Their younger siblings. Take Clutier, for example, with a population 354 in 1940 and state champs in 1942. Their head coach, John Schoenfelder, recalled what happened next: "In 1942 when Clutier won the state championship after an undefeated season, the fifth-grade girls were trying their luck on outdoor baskets. With overcoats, stocking caps, overshoes, and mittens keeping out the severe cold, they were laying the foundation for our future teams. Before school, at recess, at noon, and after school, they were outside trying to hit the basket. Since the boys would smother most of the set shots, the girls had to shoot on the run. They had heard much about rebounding while watching the high school girls scrimmage. They, too, would get the rebound and make the rebound shots."

That recollection came in the 1948 *Iowa Girls Basketball Yearbook*, when several of those fifth-grade girls, then playing for him at Clutier, took their team to state.

Teams were iconic, and state champions were celebrated in numbers that extended well beyond any reasonable

expectation for the populations of the towns, which produced those title-winning squads. Wellsburg, which had a
population of 744, took home the state title in 1949. Their
caravan home was interrupted by 2,000 fans 30 miles
from Wellsburg in Marshalltown, who demanded speeches
from some of the winning players. The caravan of cars to
greet them when they arrived home stretched for six miles.
The school with 83 students total and just 36 of them girls
had beaten 640 other teams to win the title.

By 1950 the state tournament took in north of $84,000,
and more than one million fans watched Iowa girls basketball regular-season, sectional, or state tournament games that
season alone. Greater skills, shooting, and finesse in avoiding tie-ups led to a higher-scoring title game: Slater 65,
Kamrar 52. *The Des Moines Register*, particularly Jack North,
who'd started his career covering men's sports but became a
fierce advocate for the high school girls game, began leading
the charge on coverage in the 1930s, but by this time it was
the tournament helping to promote sales of newspapers and
increasing listenership of radio stations who covered girls
basketball all around the state.

And in 1951 when Hansell defeated Monona 70–59,
Iowa was ready to begin exporting its great game aided by
a new technology. Those surprised by the television ratings
enjoyed by Iowa, then the Indiana Fever, during the Caitlin

Clark Era needed only to consult with WOI-TV director Bob Scarpino. The Ames station had been approached by the IGHSAU because once again the tournament had sold out, and many other fans wanted to watch the games. The work to send the remote signal 40 miles from Des Moines to Ames had never been attempted before. In fact, no high school game of any kind had ever been televised in Iowa.

With two minutes to airtime, the engineers successfully connected the signal. And fate took a hand as well—a snowstorm actually helped increase the power of the television signal into nine states, likely from a process called ducting. An estimated 160,000 people saw the 1951 Iowa state tournament, and WOI was flooded with calls and letters effusively thanking them for their service. By 1953 10 radio stations across the state broadcast play by play of every game, and WHO-TV in Des Moines began broadcasting the tournament in 1955, the year it moved to Veterans' Memorial Auditorium, a bigger arena. In 1956 the tournament sold more tickets in the same venue than a young singer who came to town: Elvis Presley. By the 1960s several other states broadcast the Iowa state tournament as well. And Scarpino, who died in 2020, went on to direct broadcasts of the tournament for 54 years. Even as the game itself kept developing, Iowa girls basketball had officially gone national.

CHAPTER TWO

Caitlin Clark and the Balance of Power

In 2024 Caitlin Clark broke women's basketball. She broke it in ways it desperately needed to be broken, and she shattered the ability of so many—both those steeped in the game and the millions of newcomers she brought to the previously niche space. Clark received the kind of fame that the women's game had never seen. This happened due to a perfect confluence of events; some immediately preceding Clark's rise, others a century in the making. It bizarrely sent many people seeking a single answer for what felt inexplicable. This all took place within an informational and cultural landscape quick to reach for the fast answer, eager to embrace a narrative of hero or villain, and seemingly push back hardest against the undeniably quantifiable.

And there in the eye of the hurricane, preternaturally calm, stood Clark. The very circumstances of her life dictated her path to an extent she still may not fully realize. The women's basketball moment, the growth and platform and landscape, would have found a hero, an outlet for this excitement, but Iowa itself provided a model for how it would look and sound and resonate. That Clark grew up amid this landscape, where almost everything she came to experience on a global scale was virtually normal in Iowa, both helped inform her approach to this unimaginable level of fame, inured her to the pressure, and allowed her to nurture her remarkable, still-nascent gifts without a single public misstep, an outburst, or even a stray comment that her legion of detractors, thirsting to take down the very figure who had lifted women's basketball in ways that destroyed myths about the game, could grab on to. That so many of these detractors could be found within the fabric of the game itself, too, was confounding.

But these were the extreme and often conflicting emotions that Clark's 2024 produced in virtually everyone, a magnetic disturbance, which altered the reality of so many people that when they simply attempted to reckon with it, to speak on it, their words made no sense. Somehow, through all of that: this never happened to Clark, who turned just 22 years old shortly after 2024 began. The unblemished hero of her own rise, she somehow again and again altered the trajectory of her own career, those around her, an entire league, multiple levels of her sport, and ultimately, the larger culture itself.

For example, several decades since the WNBA began play in 1997, the summer schedule of the league would run through the fall, leaving pro women's basketball with a problem: how can the teams and players command attention of the sports public in the majority of months when the league is dark? Indeed, it was a thorny issue, which multiple league presidents spoke about aloud. Donna Orender played in the first-ever women's college basketball game at Madison Square Garden in 1975 but never figured out how to take the larger audiences, television and in-person, of the women's college game and transport them into WNBA arenas. Laurel Richie, who served as WNBA president from 2011 to 2015, hoped that the attention from multiple USA Basketball Olympic gold medal teams would translate to additional WNBA attention for those same players. It didn't happen on her watch, nor did it happen in the three-year tenure of Lisa Borders from 2016 to 2018. Borders said in an exit interview for a story in *The New York Times* that she considered the long-term best-case scenario for WNBA franchises to be owned by non-NBA owners and playing in arenas seating 8,000-to-10,000 fans max.

Borders' successor is Cathy Engelbert. In a redesigned job she took on in August 2019, she is now the commissioner of the WNBA with expanded powers. And, notably, the very first thing she did as commissioner of note was to negotiate a collective bargaining agreement, signed in January 2020, which attacked this attention deficit as the central feature of the new deal. In exchange for significant increases in salary, players agreed to what was loosely called "prioritization"—a gradually more restrictive offseason, requiring them to report to camp rather than in season or lose the chance to play in the WNBA at all.

Here's how Engelbert explained it to those of us gathered to speak with her prior to Game One of the 2022 WNBA Finals: "As everyone knows, the owners really stepped up on the compensation side for the players in this collective bargaining cycle, and I think the quid pro quo for that was prioritization—showing up on time for our season. Quite frankly after 36 years in my working world, there was never once where I wasn't required to show up on time. So I think the owners were very steadfast in their commitment. For our veterans, we want them to come back and be with the team and build the chemistry that's needed to build a championship culture. I think that was something the owners really stepped up and was really important to them, and I support them wholeheartedly in that. But we understand players are going to make the best decisions for them and their families. We see that time and again."

Certainly, the logic is airtight. It also reflects an inherent belief in building a floor as opposed to a ceiling, a cautious outlook reflective of a league that had at that point gone 14 years without expanding but had multiple teams fold or abandon markets in its recent history, including in ways that must still keep James Dolan up at night as he gave up on New York itself as a women's basketball market, costing himself hundreds of millions of dollars. Still, what is most noteworthy here is that the most forward-thinking process the owners and players alike came up with was eliminating the biggest problem facing the league: when games weren't happening, people weren't paying attention. And while this change undeniably kept the current WNBA players in the public eye more—additional efforts kept WNBA players stateside, including league and team marketing deals—several other factors opened up the pipeline for fans already showing up for the college game to do the same for the pros.

While men's college basketball had enjoyed national coverage and broadcasts of its entire tournament for decades, it was not until 2019–20 that ESPN finally made the decision to do the same for the women's tournament following an 8 percent increase in ratings for the sold-out 2019 Women's Final Four. Naturally, COVID-19 immediately postponed that plan for a year. But beginning with the 2021 NCAA Tournament, all of America could watch the entirety of the drama unfold. An impressive 1.6 million people watched two freshmen, Caitlin Clark and Paige Bueckers, face off in the Sweet 16, and Bueckers came out on top in the first of two matchups between the generational guards.

When it was over, UConn head coach Geno Auriemma pulled Clark aside during the handshake line at the Alamodome in San Antonio. "He was pretty much just like, 'You're crazy good, whatnot, things like that," Clark said with a bashful smile, speaking to reporters following the game. "He's like, 'It's kind of a shame it had to be so much pressure on you and Paige. I could tell you guys were so antsy in the first half,' which I think is kind of true. I think we could feel that pressure in a way. I took a few poor shots. I think we both kind of calmed down there in the second half. Obviously, it is a lot of pressure for two freshmen. Those are the games we want to play in. Those are the moments we live for. We wouldn't want it to change any other way. To have him come up to me and say the things he did, he said, 'What you've done for Iowa this season really has been something special. You have a bright future.' To hear him say that to me really meant something. To take the time to wave me down and talk to me obviously meant a lot, and I'm very thankful for that."

Ratings for the national title game jumped to 4.1 million in 2021 up from 3.7 million in 2019. The WNBA Finals experienced a 23 percent jump, too—but to just an average of 547,000 compared to 2020's 447,000 per game and 2019's 386,000 per game. That sizable gap persisted.

But the 2021 NCAA Tournament also marked a critical turning point in how women's college basketball would be turned loose, freed of self-imposed shackles by the NCAA. Sedona Prince's social media posts documented things like the shameful gap in weight room facilities for men and women, and that launched an internal review by the NCAA, which ultimately determined that decisions like refusing to allow its own tournament to use March Madness branding, keeping that exclusively for the men, and designating the Men's Final Four as "The Final Four" on logos, labeling the women's Final Four "Women's Final Four," and providing only the men's teams who win games in the men's NCAA Tournament a stipend for doing so were all deeply self-defeating acts. Yes, it took an external law firm, Kaplan Hecker & Fink, to uncover these truths in sufficiently embarrassing a fashion that the NCAA was forced to act on things like being shocked in truly Captain Renault fashion that it spent three times as much money on the 2019 men's NCAA Tournament as it did the women's tournament that year.

By 2023 the women's tournament began utilizing March Madness branding as well. Games for the women were advertised during men's games and vice versa. By 2024 the WNBA made the decision to advertise itself during the Women's NCAA Tournament for the very first time. Its ad campaign centered around the rookie class about to join the league headlined by, of course, Clark. And wouldn't you know it? Aided by the magic ingredients of minimum levels of investment, the ability of people to watch easily, and the product treating itself like it mattered, the NCAA Women's Tournament reached another galaxy in audience. A total of 4.9 million people watched UConn–South Carolina in the 2022 final. Clark and Iowa in the 2023 final, though, saw that number increase to 9.9 million. That game was won by Angel Reese and LSU in a performance that launched an infinite number of half-baked takes and a rivalry that carried over into the WNBA. In 2024 that same matchup in the Elite Eight was watched by 12.3 million people.

The progress was happening so fast that the same folks who had repeatedly failed the women's game, but still stood to profit massively from its growth, couldn't adjust fast enough. The instruments were failing. Just a few months earlier in January 2024, the NCAA signed a long-term deal with ESPN to continue televising the tournament through 2032. The Kaplan Hecker & Fink report had estimated that the rights annually for the women's tournament should be between $81 and $112 million—*in 2021*. Again, for those keeping score at home, that came a few months after freshmen year Clark and Bueckers drew an audience of 1.6 million people. This deal was signed in January 2024, just before the entire Sweet 16 averaged 2.4 million viewers per game.

But somehow the NCAA only received a valuation of $65 million per year for the women's tournament, and NCAA president Charlie Baker pushed back, almost scoffing, at the idea that the women's tournament should approach anything close to the $880 million per year the NCAA receives for the television rights to the men's tournament. "Don't undervalue that men's tournament," Baker said to me in January 2024. "That men's tournament averages nine-and-a-half million viewers in 30 windows over 30 days. There's no other athletic event in the country that delivers the number of eyeballs that one does over the course of a 30-day period. It's completely different than basically almost everything else."

Two months later, the women's national title game between Clark's Iowa and South Carolina drew 18.9 million viewers. The men's national title game between Connecticut and Purdue? 14.8 million. "It's unfortunate to me in some ways if there's disappointment with the valuation of the tournament at $65 million because of a maybe an inflated expectation on our evaluation that was done a couple of years ago," NCAA senior vice president of basketball Dan Gavitt said when I asked him about the gap between the men's and women's valuations in January 2024. "After doing a lot of due diligence with media experts, that was flawed in many ways because of too much emphasis on affiliate fees and inflated valuation because of that. The reality is that basketball championship just a few years ago was valued independently at $6 or $7 million a year. And now just four years later is valued at 10 times that amount."

In fact, it is now obvious the media experts the NCAA spoke to had also severely undersold the audience for the tournament. Still, the NCAA chose to take that bar and pick the under. And while the rise was felt across the NCAA Tournament, the largest of those audiences again and again came to watch Clark.

The earliest signs that this newly awakened, activated group would be traversing the previously forbidden path from college to pro women's basketball—all because the highway now existed with a beacon in Clark leading the way—came from how quickly Clark games for the Indiana Fever were selling out both at home and on the road. In one of those 10,000-seat arenas Borders once said would be the perfect size for the WNBA, the Connecticut Sun quickly sold out their home opener—and Clark's pro debut—for the first time. ESPN still wasn't ready for what was about to happen. It showed the game on ESPN2, and 2.1 million people watched.

Six networks broadcast WNBA games in 2024: ABC, CBS, ESPN, ESPN2, Ion, and NBA TV. The all-time record for TV ratings in a single game for each of the six is now held by Clark.

No WNBA game had been watched by more than one million people since 2008. Twenty-three WNBA games topped one million viewers in 2024. Clark played in 20 of them. She tripled the all-time record for viewers of a WNBA All Star Game, quadrupled the record for viewers of a WNBA Draft—literally an administrative league function with everyone in evening wear. As her season unfolded with all the struggles, adjustments, and outside noise, the audience did not grow weary of the novelty. The NBA TV record she set for most viewers, she re-set eight times. The final time, a game against the Las Vegas Aces, outperformed every single NBA game on NBA TV in the men's league's 2023–24 season.

But the surest sign of Clark's durability as an icon, the way in which she has commanded and changed the balance of power in the larger culture, came after her season ended with a loss in the first round of the WNBA playoffs to the Sun.

Let's just take a stroll through some headlines on a late-December 2024 day, one in which the WNBA normally wouldn't have been mentioned, let alone had any of its players lead any stories. Free agency wasn't set to begin for another month. "Caitlin Clark supports boyfriend Connor McCaffery at Butler game in his first season as assistant coach," the *New York Post* blasted, detailing the women's basketball star…sitting there, watching, rather than focusing on the men's basketball game between Butler and Connecticut, the defending national champion in men's NCAA basketball. "Caitlin Clark's jersey retirement in Iowa is already setting records," SBNation's Noa Dalzell reported, pointing out that the get-in price for her event raising her 22 into the Carver-Hawkeye Arena on February 2, 2025 (on 2/2, get it?) was north of $700. "Fans Convinced Caitlin Clark Is Accepting Taylor Swift's Chiefs Offer," Athlon Sports declared, revealing the ample social media chatter around the idea that, yes, Taylor Swift is likely to be at an upcoming Kansas City Chiefs game to support her boyfriend, Travis Kelce, but the real story is that perhaps Clark will be joining her there, fulfilling a pledge Swift made earlier in 2024 during her Eras Tour to take in a Chiefs game with Clark.

We learned about that detail in the third but by no means final story about Clark on a sleepy Sunday in late December through a profile written about her as part of her receiving the *Time* magazine's Athlete of the Year award in 2024. An entire subplot of the WNBA offseason revolved around these two paragraphs in Sean Gregory's story. "The weekend before our interview, Clark attended back-to-back Taylor Swift shows at Lucas Oil Stadium," he wrote. "She met Swift's mother and boyfriend, Kansas City Chiefs tight end Travis Kelce. When fans noticed her sitting in a suite, they turned around to take pictures or toss her friendship bracelets. 'People are just going crazy that I'm there,' she says. 'I thought people would be so in their own world, ready to see Taylor. And it was just completely the opposite.' Swift gave Clark four bags of Eras Tour merchandise with a note saying Clark was inspiring to watch from afar. She said 'Trav and I' were excited to get to a Fever game now that the tour was winding down and invited Clark to attend a Chiefs game with her."

Let's just take a second here to note: at an Eras Tour stop, among Swifties, Clark was the one drawing attention from Swifties, the most famously loyal fanbase in the world and, yes, from Taylor Swift herself. And months later during the period the WNBA has spent decades trying to fix, Clark is still bringing attention—positive attention built around fans flocking to her at all times—to the WNBA.

Clark broke women's basketball. In the best possible way here. But also in ways that are deeply confounding to Clark and those around here. Sheila Johnson, co-owner of the WNBA's Washington Mystics, appeared on CNN and slammed *Time* for featuring Caitlin Clark as its athlete of the year. No, really. That happened. "We read *Time* magazine where Caitlin Clark was named Athlete of the Year," Johnson said on December 13. "Why couldn't they have put the whole WNBA on that cover and said the WNBA is the League of the Year because of all the talent that we have? Because when you just keep singling out one player, it creates hard feelings."

Where to start? This is, of course, sports. There are winners and losers every year, every day, in individual awards, in team accolades. The concept of fairness dictating any man in sports history being honored as Athlete of the Year simply would not be a matter of even basic debate.

But this is part of the calibration problem. There have been, as Johnson correctly noted, "so many talented players who have been unrecognized." There have been, as Risa Isard and Nicole Melton documented in their landmark September 2021 study of race in WNBA coverage by ESPN, CBS Sports, *Sports Illustrated*, and, as exhibited in WNBA team and league press releases, a disproportionate number of stories about White players compared to the majority Black makeup of the league during the 2020 season.

That study did not, however, include Clark nor does it even study the time period in which Clark has been playing college basketball or in the WNBA. It speaks to a truth that is absolutely accepted by a broad base of experts on the subject—that the WNBA's best players have been undercovered historically, and that overwhelmingly the WNBA's best players, just as a majority of all its players, have been Black.

Simple reasoning has been assigned in so many of the loudest, least-illuminating conversations about exactly why Clark is so prominent in the larger American sports culture now and what it means about both what came before her and the future of women's basketball. The more singular the explanation, the less useful it is. Even worse are the simple motivations assigned to those on both sides of this discussion. For reference, a significant number of people, particularly those with the most invested in the space, such as players, coaches, and executives, don't even view this discussion as one with opposing sides.

But for many of the harshest critics of Clark, it was easy to hear the undercurrent of fear, that the full appreciation for the women's game had come too late for them, the money which follows such fandom simply not trickling down into the sport's remarkable and compelling past. The WNBA had existed as a safe space for marginalized people for nearly three decades because broader American culture so often ignored it. That tradeoff was felt in ways large and small that filled the league's players, coaches, executives, and long-tenured fans with ambivalence. Everyone with a stake in the league's success was living in that gray area, and not only was the money too good to approach it any other way—with it the chance to finally see what a fully vested WNBA looks like—but also the momentum was so overwhelming that the league and its stakeholders couldn't stop this train if they wished to do so.

And countless often anonymous newcomers to the women's basketball space saw Clark being tested like all rookies but only clocked it through the race of the players in the majority Black league doing it, discounting all the incredible stories and women who created the scaffolding of possibility for Clark while engendering bitterness, fear, and anger. And everyone involved in this oversimplification suffered from a failure not just of understanding the racial, gender, historical, and competitive context but so often a failure in understanding that when Clark had opened these doors to the broader audience, it represented a chance for others to follow her. Clark did it first but was doing it in a way that was precisely designed for the opposite of Clark existing as a one-off phenomenon. She was a beginning, not a culmination.

And none of this means that Clark is being overcovered now. If it is true that Sue Bird, for instance, received disparate media coverage relative to her greatness or compared to, say, Sylvia Fowles—the former I'd argue is debatable; the latter is not, as the final seasons of the league's best-ever point guard in Bird and best-ever center in Fowles received deeply unequal treatment across television broadcasts and column inches alike—it did not lead to the kind of dramatic leaps in audience we have seen from Clark in 2024.

Clark is different. And there is no counterfactual in the current game: we cannot know what would have happened if Clark had been Black, built her fanbase and audience at Iowa, then taken her precision passing and 30-footers to the WNBA. But we do have a historical comp. Frequently, the comparison is made between Clark and her rivalry with Reese and the elevation of the NBA during Magic Johnson and Larry Bird's ascension from college basketball to the pros. After all, more than 35 million people watched the Michigan State–Indiana State national championship game in 1979 featuring the two stars, and the NBA reached a dramatic new level of popularity by the end of their careers.

The problem is that, unlike with Clark, it didn't happen anything like right away. (There are other problems with this comparison, too: Magic and Bird were both immediate stars of contending teams. Bird's Boston Celtics won 61 games, and Magic's Los Angeles Lakers won it all, while Reese's stardom did not translate into a playoff appearance for the Chicago Sky.) The NBA Finals remained on tape delay broadcast several seasons into both of their pro careers. The clinching win by Johnson's Lakers in the 1980 NBA Finals was preempted by many CBS network affiliates in favor of *The Incredible Hulk*, *The Dukes of Hazzard*, and *Dallas*.

By 1984 CBS showed just 10 NBA national games all regular season long. But the actual comp here for Clark also entered the league in 1984, coinciding with TBS purchasing the rights to a national TV cable package. That's Michael Jordan. Within two years a dramatic expansion of games and even the slam dunk contest—plus Jordan—helped a rising tide of NBA ratings. Jordan's Chicago Bulls helped to lead the way. To this day the four most-watched NBA Finals of all time took place in the 1990s, and they all featured Jordan's Bulls. Those ratings fell after Jordan retired—only starting to approach them once more when LeBron James reached the apex of his rivalry with Steph Curry in 2016 and 2017.

James was honored with the *Time* 2020 Athlete of the Year. The apex of these viewership trends correlate not to a generic rising tide. It is when deeply compelling stars make games must-watch TV. That is the company Clark finds herself in after a single season. The audience tells us so. *Time* only has been naming an Athlete of the Year since 2019, but *Sports Illustrated* has honored someone in this way since 1954. In 1991? It was Jordan. If there are any contemporaneous accounts of anyone suggesting the entire

NBA should have received the award instead of Jordan in 1991 or James in 2020, I was unable to find them.

When Johnson's Mystics won the WNBA title in 2019, playing home games in a sold-out but entirely-too-small 4,200-seat Entertainment and Sports Arena, or ESA, she celebrated her team with, among other things, a massive championship ring. According to the Mystics' press release: "Adorning the ring top is the Mystics DC logo set with custom-cut rubies and sapphires. Combined, the six custom-cut sapphires and six custom-cut rubies are symbolic of the 12 players on the team's roster with the singular round sapphire representing head coach Mike Thibault. The iconic logo is set atop the WNBA Championship Trophy, which features six diamonds in its base signifying the incredible six total games won by the Mystics in the 2019 playoffs as well as one larger diamond at the top, which pays tribute to their first-ever championship victory. Surrounding the trophy and logo are 23 diamonds. An encircling ring of 29 taper-cut rubies represent the 26 regular-season wins and the three games won in the Finals. Completing the ring top are an additional 90 diamonds and the team's title of '2019 WNBA CHAMPIONS.' The top and bottom edges of the ring top are accented with 8 princess-cut sapphires for a combined total of 16 sapphires. The eight princess-cut sapphires are symbolic of the Mystics' new home court advantage in DC's Ward 8. The Mystics compiled an 18–3 record at the Entertainment and Sports Arena, including the decisive Game Five of the WNBA Finals."

Only the Mystics, the team that won the title, received this ring. Not the entire WNBA.

And in 2024 the Mystics moved four home games from ESA to Capital One Arena, where the NBA's Washington Wizards play. One of those games, with Reese's Chicago Sky, drew 10,000 fans. Another with Diana Taurasi and Brittney Griner's Phoenix Mercury drew 12,586. The other two against Caitlin Clark and the Fever drew 20,333 and 20,711. Put another way: Clark's two visits to play the Mystics in 2024 drew 41,044 fans, almost half of what Washington's entire 2023 home slate drew: 87,813 fans. "There were so many times where it felt like if a call was made against the other team, people were cheering, which typically in an away environment, you're not getting positive feedback from the crowd," Clark's Fever teammate, Lexie Hull, said. "But this year that happened several places, so feel very fortunate about that."

But how does one reconcile it all? It's complicated, and evaluating the ways in which race has held the league back, and acting and appreciating the progress that has followed through that prism, is not the same thing as pretending it isn't happening at all or that the league as a whole is not benefiting from Clark's ability to maximize this moment made possible by pioneers in her home state and trailblazers in the WNBA alike. Bad-faith actors have entered the WNBA space intent on using Clark's presence like a club to attack Black women of the league while at the same time embracing how many new fans have arrived to love and appreciate her and so many others in the WNBA. And it puts extra pressure on her opponents, who are forced to simultaneously answer a disproportionate amount of questions about a player who isn't even on their own team in most cases. But if that effort leads to a foul deemed unnecessary by Clark's vociferous fanbase—with the ugliest manifestations of that passion curdled by racism—players were subjected to cruel, inhuman taunts, even death threats.

Every bit of that discordant mix is something Clark is hyper aware of. She is the calm in this sea of madness, able to hold two disparate ideas in her head at the same time in ways that so many, who are paid to analyze, failed at verbalizing all year long. Each of these failures from someone with a megaphone only further complicates the degree of difficulty for Clark, her teammates, and her opponents alike, ratcheting up the tension further. "I tell people I feel like the most controversial person," Clark told *Time*. "But I am not. It's just because of all the storylines that surround me.

I literally try to live and treat everybody in the same exact respectful, kind way. It just confuses me at times."

And here is Clark, being asked to navigate all of it while playing basketball against the best competition in the world, answering endless questions from the media, and working to make time for every fan who she encounters on sidelines and in restaurants and in any casual setting around the country, to parse every word in a country so hopelessly divided, criticized for anything she might say and even anything she might not say—all at the age of 22. She attempted several times to speak on this during the season at places ill-suited for nuanced conversations about race in America. Scripted and at events designed for them to speak, politicians have failed to do this well in 2024 America.

Clark was asked to do it, surrounded by portable microphones, still in uniform just after basketball practice. But by the offseason, she'd had a chance to gather her thoughts. "I want to say I've earned every single thing, but as a White person, there is privilege," Clark told *Time*. "A lot of those players in the league that have been really good have been Black players. This league has kind of been built on them. The more we can appreciate that, highlight that, talk about that, and then continue to have brands and companies invest in those players that have made this league incredible, I think it's very important. I have to continue to try to change that.

The more we can elevate Black women, that's going to be a beautiful thing."

Her parents, Brent and Anne, have built a protective shield around her as much as they can. She is ably represented by Erin Kane and Excel. But the life of the most famous athlete in the WNBA, and one of the most recognized athletes in the world, involves answering questions before and after every game, at every practice. Every move on the court is broadcast and recorded in high-definition, any misstep taken to social media and endlessly repeated forever. That she managed to survive her first year absent anything approaching the kind of verbal live-ball turnover that would have turned the Clark news cycle against her only helped her further amass the power no women's basketball player has ever enjoyed.

This was perhaps never clearer than when Clark in November of 2024…played golf. Specifically, the ANNIKA, a Pro-Am event, added Clark to their assembled talent of the best players in the world and famous amateur golfers alike. None, though, more famous than Clark, who'd grown up playing everything. But when she was asked by reporters back at her exit interview, following the end of her WNBA season, what she most wanted to do in the offseason, she said she wanted focus on her golf game, earning joking caution from Fever teammate Aliyah Boston.

She'd started playing with a pink set of clubs, begging Brent to take her golfing any weekend she had off from basketball or soccer. He'd often oblige. In college she and a teammate would usually play in a foursome against a pair of male Hawkeye student managers. The stakes were nothing more than the ability to, as Clark put it, "talk crap the next day at practice." But this? This was a different level. Clark played her first nine holes with 15-time LPGA event winner Nelly Korda and the back nine with the event's namesake, Annika Sorenstam. "It's great that [Clark is] here, very thankful to her to take the time to be part of our event," Sorenstam said that day to gathered reporters. "She's a really nice person, down to Earth. She's an athlete. You can tell. If she didn't hit it well, she's a little bit upset because she knows she can do it. She just doesn't play a lot. She has some power off the tee. It's wonderful of the fans come out here and support her. It's great for the tour."

The Golf Channel altered its entire broadcast schedule, moving its signature highlight show *Golf Today* 90 minutes earlier for the chance to broadcast Clark's 18th hole live. But amid the attention, Clark had the presence of mind not to lose the joy of the moment, even though her presence at the event meant she was advancing in the sports world, excelling on the court, and representing basketball off of it in ways that simultaneously were growing the space and creating chances for her and those who come after her, too. Her empathy amid her closed circle and deeply examined day-to-day life was almost impossible to fathom from someone so young. "I remind myself, like I don't really care what happens," Clark said, smiling, sitting next to Sorenstam and answering reporters' questions the day before the event. "Doesn't really matter. I don't play golf for a living, just have fun with it. This isn't super serious. Enjoy the experience. There were so many people that would kill to be in my position or in my shoes. The people following outside the ropes would love an opportunity to hit a ball on the first tee or something like that. So just remind yourself how cool this experience is and don't let it pass you by. I think that's anything I do in life. Whatever I get to do and the opportunities I have, soak it in. A lot of people would trade and want to have these opportunities as well."

And the notorious trash talker also couldn't help pointing out that her Fever teammate, Grace Berger, still hadn't played golf with her despite Berger's status as state champion while playing for Sacred Heart High School in Kentucky. "Actually, one of my teammates was a state champion golfer, so she's pretty good," Clark said. "I actually haven't played with her yet. I think she might be scared or something. I don't know why. Her game must have gotten rusty when she became a professional basketball player."

Berger saved her reply for the comments in Clark's Instagram post: "If I hadn't seen the video of the shank, these photos would've convinced me that you could beat me."

And the fun back and forth all led to coverage in places that never paid much attention to the WNBA even during the season and completely ignored it in the offseason.

When Clark finished at 18, a group of LPGA pros were waiting to take photos with her, followed by a swarm of autograph requests by assembled fans. She'd even imported the jersey swap from basketball, and she and Korda traded jerseys after her practice round the day before. Ticket sales were up significantly, according to the tournament's organizers. "I witnessed the Caitlin Clark Effect. That's for sure," the best analog to Clark in women's golf, Rose Zhang, said after her second round that week. "I was able to talk to her a little bit right before she left actually. She's just such an incredible role model for young players both on the basketball court and also on the golf course. We as professional golfers are constantly inspired by her presence, her ability to just make things fun, and make a lot of the people watch women's sports. So the fact that she came here—and there were more people in a pro-am than an actual golf tournament—says a lot."

It is that last part that no one has ever seen before—a women's basketball player dictating the terms of engagement throughout the larger culture. No one is asking Clark to save women's basketball. Those in the space already felt the tailwinds behind the growth that both preceded Clark and helped fuel her own rise. Clark taking over the sports world in 2024 would not have been possible otherwise. Those who preceded her in the previous century would not benefit from the landscape of 2024 the way she did. She is a product of her time no more or less than Dorcas Andersen was of hers. Had Andersen been born 10 years earlier, she wouldn't have enjoyed the opportunity to travel to Des Moines and dominate the state tournament because that tournament didn't yet exist. Had Andersen been born 10 years later, she might have come into this world too late to start Audubon High School down a path of dominance that led her coach, M.M. McIntire, to preserve girls basketball as an institution.

Did Andersen save girls basketball in Iowa? Or did girls basketball in Iowa create the path for success enjoyed by Andersen? Did Clark revolutionize the way women's basketball could be played? Or did the specific evolution of the Iowa girls game, consistent competition, and the focus on pinpoint passing and long-range shooting pioneered by the smallest teams to win Iowa state championships design a template for the Caitlinball played by Lisa Bluder, Jan Jensen, and Iowa, and now the Indiana Fever? Did Clark elevate women's basketball to unprecedented heights in 2024 in ways no player ever has? Or did the rising tide of women's basketball built by generations of stars, who received but a tiny fraction of the attention Clark gets in a day, make what Clark did possible? The answer to all of it is yes.

CHAPTER THREE

The Hornettes Change the Game

By the dawn of the 1960s, girls basketball in Iowa had become an immovable institution. "Girls basketball is as much a part of our state as our green valley of corn," Iowa governor Herschel Loveless declared in 1958. That'll happen when three generations are given the chance to experience girls basketball: the 1952 champion, Reinbeck, featured Jean Shoup, whose mother Grace Hoepner Shoup (1929–32) and grandmother Alvina Mull Hoepner (1911) all played high school basketball. (When Jean died in 2023, it was the first accomplishment listed in a long, full life. Her obituary said she "cherished that memory.")

Bowing to the popularity of the six-on-six game, larger school districts in Iowa began sponsoring girls teams as well even as the pressure on smaller school districts to consolidate led to a reduction in the total number of girls basketball teams participating each year. More broad opportunities but fewer spots meant that the balance began to shift toward Iowa's larger municipalities. The rule changes, too, had practical effects. The game sped up in 1934, when the three-court setup—girls were not permitted to leave one of their three zones, and there were two girls to a zone—evolved into the longtime two-court, three girls to a zone setup that most people associate with six-on-six basketball as they knew it for the better part of 60 years in Iowa.

By the 1950s a pair of new regulations offered new strategic opportunities for coaches who could exploit them. One was the widening of the lane, where players were only permitted to remain for three seconds, further limiting the long-standing strategic advantage to the Iowa schools "that one year when they happened to have the tallest girl or the best shooter," as *The Des Moines Register*'s John Carlson put it in 1999. Regardless of where she stood on the court, no girl could hold the ball for more than three seconds either. And tie-ups were only permitted in the act of shooting or in the lane. (This last one would turn out to be particularly important.)

In the fall of 1960, 22-year-old Larry Wiebke, fresh out of Upper Iowa University with his teaching degree, rolled into Van Horne, Iowa, in "a brand new, cheapest Chevrolet I could buy" to begin working as a physical education teacher and girls basketball coach at Van Horne High School. "I thought I was on top of the world," he told me, though he had no idea he was about to change the course of Iowa basketball forever and do so in just two years' time.

Van Horne is in Benton County, about seven miles from Newhall, where Melba Gardemann Olsen found glory winning the 1927 title. The town's population, as of the census taken the year Wiebke arrived, stood at 554, not dramatically different from 1900's 484 or 2020's 774. Wiebke's first sport was baseball. A three-time letter winner in it at Upper Iowa, he also played basketball at UIU. He was not especially bonded to girls basketball. He and his UIU roommate arrived in Van Horne and discussed the matter. Wiebke's roommate preferred to coach the boys, so he took the girls.

Van Horne suffered from a problem of geography that kept the Hornettes out of the state tournament year after year. To even reach the state tournament meant winning county honors first, and in Benton County a powerhouse stood in their way of doing that even during their best seasons. Garrison High School was coached by legendary Ben Corbett, who led the Rockettes to the 1957 state title.

Still, in his first year coaching Van Horne in 1960–61, Wiebke noticed immediately that, though his team lacked stature with only one girl taller than 5'5", he had some key advantages he could utilize. "They were quick, and they were accurate in their passing," Wiebke said in a telephone interview in September 2024. "Their passing game was unbelievable. You see a movie or a film of them. You see the ball going out of their hands to somebody else, and then you all of a sudden, you wouldn't see anything, and—bingo—the other person would have it."

The connectivity of the team also manifested itself in superior screening. That was a vital part of the Van Horne offense, which allowed just enough room behind a defender for the undersized Hornettes to get their shots off. The reason those six players—Mickey Schallau, Marla Heitman, her cousin Jo Heitman, Evelyn Brehm, Marjorie Dutton, and Jean Garbers—played so well together is that they'd all been playing together since they were in fifth grade.

"The girls that played together with this championship team, we were all friends in a small school, right? And we're still friends," Brehm said by phone in September 2024. "It just was never jealousy or anything like that among the six of us because we were just such good friends. We did things together off the court, too."

A consistent theme within generations of Iowa girls basketball came from championing the player as a whole person. The best coaches—even the ones known for their high standards—took particular note of prioritizing other activities as well, and the Iowa Girls High School Athletic Union (IGHSAU) met every year with their corresponding numbers in music and other extracurricular activities to create after-school schedules collaboratively.

As Karen Kanke James recorded them back in 1962, here are brief portraits of the six Van Horne starters: "Marjorie Dutton is a daughter of Dr. and Mrs. D.A. Dutton and active in Y.F. and the music program of the EUB church. She is a member of the school band and mixed chorus, sings in quartets and sextettes, and contributes her musical talents to school music programs. She also has won honors in declamatory contests, plays softball, and is a member of the Industrious Union 4 H Club.

"Evelyn Brehm is the daughter of Herman Brehm, president of the Van Horne school board. She has been a state winner in the Legion oratorical contest, member of the winning Benton County 4H demonstration team, winner in declamatory contests, and has held all offices in the Industrious Union 4H club and taken many honors in 4H. She loves to cook and sew, is a member of the school band, and sings in the glee club and mixed chorus. Upon graduation she plans to enter the University of Iowa and will major in political science.

"Marla Heitman is active in Y.F. and Sunday school of the EUB Church, is editor of the school paper, attended a two-week journalism workshop at the University of Iowa this past summer, has taken part in declamatory contests, likes to write and paint pictures by number, and, when not in school, helps her dad drive a tractor on their farm three-and-a-half miles north of Van Horne. The past two summers, she has detasseled corn. Her parents are the Wilbert Heitmans.

"Jo Ann Heitman, daughter of the Donald Heitmans, who live north and west of Van Horne, attended the journalism workshop with her cousin, Marla. She is treasurer and secretary of the student council, active in Walther League at St. Andrew's Lutheran church, belongs to the 4H Grove Producers 4H and Big feeds calves. She is editor of the school annual, plays softball on the team, and helps her father on the farm.

"Jean Garbers, daughter of the Henry Garbers, is president of the Industrious Union 4H club, member of St. Andrew's Lutheran church and of the Walther League, and secretary-treasurer of the senior class. She sings in mixed chorus and girls glee club, is a member of the school band, has participated in declamatory contests, and is on the school softball team. She enjoys helping her father on the farm—often drives the tractor—and she loves to cook. She will enter Drake University this fall. She loves all sports, but basketball is her favorite."

After losing a spot in the state tournament to Alburnett to end their junior season, Brehm and her friends knew they had only one more chance at the goal they'd all talked about endlessly, dating back to their run as seventh graders: rampaging undefeated and making it to the state tournament.

"It was a dream," Brehm said. "We got to play together, the six of us got to play together in our seventh- and eighth-grade years and so we just talked about that, getting to high school, and the dream of going to the state tournament."

But even achieving that modest goal felt beyond the tiny town with undersized players. However, Brehm scored 30 to take down HLV in the semifinals of the state qualifying tournament, and by defeating Marengo's Iowa Valley 55–49 in Oskaloosa, the Hornettes qualified as one of 16 state tournament teams. When the game went final, the Van Horne fire whistle woke the town. No one panicked, though. Everyone understood it meant their girls had reached the state tournament. Thirteen of those teams won berths by taking home a sectional title. Three others didn't have to and simply qualified by going undefeated. The latter path was how 27–0 Garrison arrived at the state tournament in March 1962. Van Horne had already faced them three times that season and lost each time.

But Wiebke understood that the gap between the two teams was less drastic than the win-loss records suggested. "The scores that they beat us by through the season kept getting less and less and less," Wiebke recalled, "three games total of 11 points. And I said, 'You know what? We could probably just turn that around and beat them by 11.' And somewhere along the line, they got the message and they played ball."

School let out early for everyone on Tuesday, March 6. Two busloads of Van Horne players, coaches, chaperones, fans, and other supporters—James said one local account estimated the number of people making the trip as "most of Benton County"—traveled the hour-plus back roads to Waterloo. The one-year divergence from playing in Des Moines was due to a previously booked national bowling tournament, a scheduling error all made sure never to happen again, choosing not to take I-380 because it hadn't been built yet. (Notably: when the IGHSAU decided to move the tournament from Veterans' Memorial Auditorium in 2005 to the Wells Fargo Arena in 2006, the Hornettes were all invited back to the tournament, honored there, and had the chance to hear Vets' cheers from more than 13,000 people. They'd been denied that opportunity by the bowling tournament 43 years before.)

But back in 1962, as they pulled up at the arena, where Jo said years later "we were just excited enough to make it; we didn't care where it was at"—they traveled straight to the venue the same day to avoid missing extra school.

The town had been waiting for them. That morning's *Waterloo Daily Courier* provided a grand welcoming. It read "Welcome Girls' State Tournament Visitors" above even the publication name on the front page, and a large page one story, adorned by a team photo of the Eldora Tigerettes, sat above the less important news of an exchange of letters between John F. Kennedy and Nikita Khrushchev. The Hornettes watched much of the action from the Bennett vs. Guthrie Center game, which preceded theirs, then headed to the locker room to change. "Our kids started out of the locker room and got to the floor, and the gal that was in charge of us could only just get us back in the locker room before the game started," Wiebke recalled with a chuckle. "They were ready to play, and they really wanted to beat Garrison."

Added team manager Karen Kanke James in her written recollections back in 1962: "There was very little excitement in the dressing room and few instructions from the coach. But you could just feel the spirit and determination."

Wiebke had become close friends with Corbett, the Garrison coach who had a more understated style of coaching. He sat on the bench, wearing his signature red socks, red shirt, and string tie, a calming influence on his players that had worked for 27 straight games. But not this time. The Hornettes took a single-digit lead into halftime, at which point the longtime friends decided it would be Brehm's time to take over. "Part of it was they were looking for me," Brehm recalled 62 years later. "But I'll tell you what: yeah, the other two gals [Mickey and Marla, the two leading scorers for Van Horne], they, they were so capable, their shooting ability and so forth. And I would call the plays.

And I mean, they depended on me to do that, right? And I never thought that I was that important for the shooting part of it."

Her modesty got the better of her recollection. But it turned out her shooting part of it was critically important. She hit the first four shots of the third quarter. The Van Horne lead ballooned to 15. The dragon had been slayed. Van Horne beat Garrison 72–57.

Somehow, the scene was entirely bereft of bitterness. Players from both teams gathered at midcourt and hugged one another. The Garrison players understood how big this was for Van Horne. Both teams had traveled the same route to get here, a cavalcade on Route 218 that, according to one of the clips James had collected, was "one continuous string, almost like a train to Benton County." Only reluctantly did the players disperse from midcourt when urged by several policemen before taking the team bus back to the Ellis Hotel. Nor did Corbett begrudge his friend Wiebke a bit. As he said that night: "Now we can say we beat the state champs three out of four times." Wiebke said when the tournament was over that the win over Garrison was key to Van Horne's entire run. "When our girls finally beat Garrison, I think they realized they could go all the way."

The road would not be easy. Bennett, their next opponent, featured two 5'11" forwards and was the top overall seed in the state entering tournament play. Wiebke had seen them up close during that first day. With all that height, coach Carroll Rugland employed a "tiger defense," the first-of-its-kind full-court press in the six-on-six game. But it was Corbett who got word to Wiebke to meet him, along with *The* (Cedar Rapids) *Gazette* sportswriter Jack Ogden, once the two coaches had settled their teams into their rooms at the Ellis and Ogden filed his column on Van Horne. When he arrived at the bar, Wiebke saw three drinks on the counter. "Let's go, Wiebke," Corbett said to him. "You're three behind."

And with that the three men stayed up, drinking and plotting how to beat Bennett. "Guys, what are we going to do against this outfit?" Wiebke recalled asking. "I said, 'You've seen us both. They have some weight on us every leg, some inches on everybody.' [Corbett] said, 'Well, you just keep doing what you're doing.' He said, 'I don't think they're used to that kind of ball.'

"And we tried it. It worked."

As Brehm added: "That's the kind of man Ben Corbett was. He was right there that night ready to help Larry."

In the locker room, a quiet confidence reigned. Schallau lightened the mood, telling her teammates: "Listen kids, win or lose, we come right back here tonight. No having to be chased off by the cops again." That night the Hornettes executed Wiebke's plan to perfection. Van Horne 59, Bennett 49.

The losing coach took it harder than Corbett did. Bennett's Rugland, only 26 years old himself at that tournament, didn't talk to his players for two days after Bennett fell to Van Horne. It took Corbett and Wiebke intervening to urge him to "cut that behavior out," as Wiebke recalled, and urged Rugland to remember all his players had accomplished. Still, Rugland's approach may have differed from Wiebke's ability, as Brehm put it, to "handle the girls where they're at" emotionally, but Rugland's success was undeniable on the court. He'd go on to win 735 games against 245 losses in 41 years at Bennett, Monteczuma, and Hampton-Dumont, reaching the state tournament 15 times. Corbett won 734 games vs. 258 losses in 31 years at Garrison and Dysart-Geneseo. Ogden has an annual award given to the best boys and girls athlete in his name for the past 41 years, while his son, J.R., is now the sports editor at his old paper, *The Gazette*.

With that Van Horne was on to the title game against Mediapolis, helmed by a relatively young head coach as well. Vernon "Bud" McLearn, just 29 years of age, was just beginning a career at Mediapolis, in which he'd coach his teams to 21 state tournaments in 28 years, finish with a lifetime record of 706–80, and defend the Mediapolis home court to the tune of a lifetime home mark of 333–8.

Mediapolis was led by Judy Amenell, a forward capable of scoring from anywhere. She put up 40 points, but the pint-sized Schallau virtually matched her with 37, and the Hornettes largely shut down the remaining Bullettes. Still, in the final minute, Van Horne led just 58–57, and Mediapolis had trapped Dutton in the backcourt. Dutton pulled a senior move, though, offering the ball to freshman Nancy Jarvis, who grabbed it. That tie-up was against the rules, leading to a technical foul. Schallau calmly sank two free throws, exiting the trouble spot on the court, and giving the Hornettes the cushion they needed to win it all. Brehm remembered that Schallau had instructed her team ahead of taking those free throws. Her instructions began with the phrase: "Now when I make it...."

"That's how confident she was," Brehm said, marveling at it 62 years later.

It was contagious. Brehm raced in and stole the subsequent inbounds pass, and shortly after that, the smallest team anyone could remember, in every measurable way, was champion of the Iowa girls basketball world.

When the final horn sounded in Waterloo, Brehm remembered not only the leaping embraces from her teammates, the six young girls who had lived a dream, but also that she could look into the stands and see her parents; her two older sisters, both married and cheering her on with their husbands; her older sister, home from college to watch; her younger brother as well; and too many cousins to count. "And then," she said, "all the other people who'd come up to me and say: 'I was there. I was at that game.'"

Wiebke's parents were on hand to watch him become the youngest coach to lead a state championship team to this day, as were his uncle, his sister, and a number of high school friends. It wouldn't hit him until a few years later just how singular an achievement it was. (Incidentally, the IGHSAU has a full video archive of the game you can watch on YouTube! It is like a portal into basketball past played like the present.)

As the team made its way to the Hotel President, a showcase hotel constructed just before the 1929 stock market crash, for a banquet to celebrate with their families, the IGHSAU, and dignitaries, including the mayor of Waterloo. Journalists present were already reckoning with what had changed irrevocably in Iowa basketball. Jack Woods wrote: "The Hornettes, averaging 5–3 in the frontcourt and 5–5 in the back court, were easily the tiniest team in the state field. But they were also the best ball handling, dribbling, and shooting team."

Driving and cutting, fast-paced pick-and-rolls, shots from anywhere, the kind of basketball that Caitlin Clark plays had been discovered that night in Waterloo to be the way championship basketball could be played. Corbett said: "It's the first time coaches have taken advantage of the wide lane and the tie-up rules to bring the smaller-but-faster girl back into play."

It is why Brehm loves watching the Iowa Hawkeyes so much, especially during the Clark years. She sees her childhood friends, her friends to this day, in the way they play. "Well, the fast break, for one thing, ours was just from the half-line, right? But we outran people with the break and the passing, the setting of screens, all of that," she said. "And I'll say, 'Oh, what a great screen.' Or I'll [feel it when] Caitlin Clark can find somebody she can thread that pass to."

Wiebke added wryly, "But none of you could make the shots from halfcourt."

Still, a new standard, a kind of play, had been set. As the opening paragraph of the 1962 *Iowa Girls Basketball Yearbook* put it: "In a game that may have spelled the death knell for the post forward style of basketball so long played by Iowa girls and brought abruptly into the spotlight the type of game your editors think will replace it, a fast-breaking band of little ones from Van Horne outscored another fast-breaking crew from Mediapolis 62–59."

Plenty of posts in the decade to come, Jan Jensen among the very best of them, would offer counterevidence to this declared death of the center. But Van Horne's success helped instruct an entire sport that winning with elite guard play wasn't just realistic, it was a necessary prerequisite in the modern game. A system that married the Van Horne Hornettes to the Jan Jensen/Dorcas Andersen big was still several decades away. But don't tell that to a coach who told a reporter the night Van Horne triumphed: "I'm going home and tell my big girl to take up the flute and forget basketball. This pass-and-cut game is here to stay."

If the celebration that greeted Van Horne's return home had been merely the size of the hubbub shown to Blakesburg, the fourth-place finishers in 1962, it would have been noteworthy. Featuring a 25-car parade led by the Blakesburg fire truck, 300 people packed a local gymnasium to cheer on the girls who brought their high school glory, the mayor feted them, and it was followed by a lunch banquet.

But that's not anywhere close to what happened when Van Horne returned home with a trophy unlike any other in their high school trophy case. Early that morning Schallau woke up and exclaimed to her still-groggy teammates: "Hey girls! We won the state tournament!"

All four semifinalists enjoyed police escorts that Sunday, but the crowd awaiting the Hornettes when they arrived at the designated starting place for the parade, at the corner of Garrison and Rt. 218, startled even them. By 1:30 PM more than 300 cars lined up to salute the Van Horne champions as they took a slow, 90-minute path to the Van Horne High School Gym. Six girls out of a graduating class of 21 in a town of 554 people produced a crowd of more than 2,000 who turned out on a gray, 36-degree day, braving intermittent sleet and snow to stand in the slush and hold up signs and cheer, then pile into the gym to cheer some more, all to celebrate the Van Horne girls basketball team's accomplishments on the court. Signs hung in store windows: "Hurrah for Van Horne." A boy of 12 or 13 wore a sign around his neck: "We're Proud of You Van Horne." And in a nod to the space race, a sign in front of Curtis' Welding: "Congratulations, Van Horne Missile Maids, You Played Space Age Ball".

Corbett was there, too, cheering on his rival. And the Garrison High School pep band played in salute to their neighbors. Emotions ran high and not just from Brehm, who declared that day from the podium set up in the gym for her team, Wiebke, and dignitaries: "We just can't believe it. When we went to the tournament, we didn't think we could win it. And it still seems like we'll have to play again next week."

At that she burst into tears. Longtime Van Horne resident and mayor Donald Kerkman didn't manage that even, saying he was "too overcome to speak."

Stories about the celebration ran in newspapers throughout Iowa in the days that followed. It is equally significant that a story in the *Waterloo Daily Courier* noted on March 13, two days after the celebration and three days after the championship game in which Brehm and Mediapolis' Joanne Breder had guarded one another, that the two girls had previously roomed together the summer before at Girls State. That was the granular level at which fans hungered for details of their stars. Weeks after the championship, mere news that the Van Horne girls team would be attending a local banquet merited a story in *The Gazette*. That is the level of coverage girls basketball in Iowa was receiving. And the crowds which followed—precursors for Caitlin Clark's experience—were no more a magic trick than Clark's are. They are, however, the blueprint.

What did not follow, in ways that Clark and her supporters can take for granted, was a potential future in basketball. And even the circumstances, which produced Van Horne's shocking title, changed quickly enough that it could never be repeated.

After she graduated Brehm enrolled at University of Iowa but found her calling in elementary education rather than political science. She returned home to Van Horne, now an adult, and reconnected with Wiebke. The two were married in 1965, and they'll celebrate their 60th wedding anniversary in 2025. A few years after their wedding, Larry and Evelyn adopted their daughter, Karen. That decision, Evelyn said matter-of-factly, meant she had to resign from teaching sixth grade, though she was permitted to continue substituting. I asked her whether that bothered her. "No, because I wanted to be at home," Brehm said. "And Larry wanted me to be at home."

Of the six Van Horne Hornettes, only Jo Heitman played beyond high school—briefly on an AAU team associated with her job at *Look* magazine—before giving that up to attend business school. Even their Mediapolis opponent, Amenell, who'd started crying when asked in the aftermath of the game whether she'd finished playing, had no place to continue her career. She did return to the Iowa state tournament in 1984, though, to cheer on her daughter, Lisa Thomas, a key contributor for her former head coach Bud McLearn with Mediapolis in 1984. The Mediapolis population—in the low four figures consistently since Amenell's time—meant the school avoided consolidation.

Wiebke coached the Van Horne girls again in 1963 in both basketball and softball but in 1964 was given a larger portfolio: Van Horne, Newhall, Blairstown, and Keystone. On July 1, 1964, the Hornettes were no more. Newhall's 1927 championship team no longer had a high school of its own either. By the end of the 1960s, consolidation had eliminated every single one-room schoolhouse in the state. Arguments raged then and now whether that was good or bad for Iowa on balance. But indisputably it was different. The 1962 trophy now resides in the Van Horne Public Library.

Wiebke was asked to continue coaching girls basketball at Benton Community High School right in Van Horne, and he did so for eight years, leading the Bobcats to a 156–39 record. He coached the softball team for 24 years, winning 650 games and earning enshrinement in the Iowa Softball Coaches Hall of Fame. But he never viewed himself as a feminist, any more than the towering figure of the IGHSAU, E. Wayne Cooley, did when he was asked that question directly. "Oh, I might be a feminist. I just never thought of that before," Cooley told journalist Chuck Offenburger in 1992. "I have fought some battles over the years to get equality for girls. When you think of it, the athletic arena was the home of men and boys for more than 200 years. Only in recent times have women and girls started coming into athletics, and sometimes they've had to overcome hostility to do it. In Iowa at least, the girl athlete can walk down the street just as tall as the boy athlete. No taller, but no shorter either."

Naturally, if Wiebke had come of age at a different moment in women's basketball history, a very different future might have presented itself. I asked him whether he ever missed it. "Well, there are days when I do and days when I don't, you know?" Wiebke replied. "Yeah, it's something that we did, we accomplished that. So there's no reason to dwell on it forever. It was just a happy day here—then forward."

Forward, yes, but not away. Wiebke and Brehm still live in the same town, going on 65 years later, that Wiebke drove into with his brand new Chevrolet. They attend Benton High School girls basketball games—"not as much as we'd like to," she said, to which Wiebke countered, "or should," though she noted Benton reached the state tournament the past three years—and are regular consumers of WNBA games. Indiana Fever broadcasts are big in their house, of course, but so were Las Vegas Aces matchups in 2024. Brehm noted that both Kate Martin and Megan Gustafson, former Iowa Hawkeyes, played for the Aces, while Kiah Stokes came from Marion. "We were so excited for Kate Martin when she got the call," Brehm said, referring to when Jan Jensen's niece, Martin, was selected in the 2024 WNBA Draft.

But Wiebke and Brehm are content in the very place that celebrated them all those years ago. "I had a couple chances to interview [for jobs] in Cedar Rapids," Wiebke said. "I didn't even accept the invitation because, hey, I like it where I am and what I'm doing. I don't think I want to get involved with something that large. So, I just stay here."

And while Brehm and Jo are still in Van Horne, the rest of the Hornettes have scattered—Marla to San Diego, Dutton to Colorado Springs, Garbers to just outside of Minneapolis, and Schallau in Peoria, Illinois. That doesn't mean they aren't still teammates, though. And they saw themselves in the Iowa teams of today, in the Caitlin Clark Hawkeyes, when they watch Iowa games as a group—together but apart—on a text chain with every starter from the 1962 Van Horne Hornettes. "We just love seeing what the Iowa girls did because that's the way they worked," Brehm said. "And that's what Lisa Bluder and her staff worked on. We text back and forth, the six of us, and comment on that all the time."

And every so often—she says it happens more around March, when the state tournament is played—Brehm finds herself closing her eyes and remembering what it felt like, sitting with those same six girls in a slow-moving school bus driving down Main Street in Van Horne, thousands of people cheering them for what they did, not even knowing what their breakthrough would mean for the generations to come.

CHAPTER FOUR

Caitlin Clark's WNBA

As has often been the case throughout her Hall of Fame career as a head coach and executive, Lin Dunn saw it all before anyone else. While the drama built during the first few months of Caitlin Clark's senior season—would the generational superstar leave college in four years or stay for a fifth, a decision made possible by the COVID-19 pandemic—Dunn saw all the factors pointing in a single direction. She'd spent the past two years building a team even as she celebrated her 75th birthday during a time when many people would have been satisfied to settle into retirement and recount their many victories.

But something about Dunn's energy, her endless capacity to talk, think about, and love women's basketball, has never let her rest. Her Indiana Fever, the team she led to a WNBA title in 2012 and spent more time with than any other employer in a career that began before Title IX reigned as the law of the land, had desperately needed her to organize and supercharge a rebuild, which had been stuck in place for half a decade. So while sitting in Gainbridge Fieldhouse the moment the ping pong balls of the lottery bounced Indiana's way, she saw every bit of the WNBA season that was to follow. "I was not shocked," Dunn said in an October 2024 phone conversation. "I was not stunned. I expected us to win the lottery, and knowing that we were going to win the lottery, then the next step was that we were going to draft Caitlin Clark. It was just a matter of fact. It was: okay, now let's get ready to work with this once-in-a-lifetime, generational point guard. And let's remember it's very hard to find those generational point guards, and so when one is on your radar, you better grab her, and you better hold on to her. Just like in the NBA, they don't come along very often. And so she is a generational point guard with a very high basketball IQ, good size. She's got the big hands, she's got all the tools, and so I just knew. *Okay, this is our next step. Now she's coming. We're gonna put her with [Aliyah] Boston and [Kelsey] Mitchell, and this is going to be the core that's going to take us back to winning championships.*"

Dunn was born May 10, 1947, and raised in Alabama before her family moved to Tennessee her junior year of high school. Despite coming from a family of athletes—her dad, Harry, ran track at Vanderbilt, while her mom, LaRue, played three-court six-on-six in high school—she had to find basketball in an ad hoc fashion due to the limitations of opportunities for women when she was growing up. "I grew up in a highly competitive family but always loved basketball," Dunn remembered. "[I] had a hoop in the backyard. I had PE teachers in junior high that influenced me because it was against the law in Alabama for girls to play interscholastic sports. I finally got to play two years of the old six-on-six way in Tennessee, and then there were no scholarships. This was way before Title IX, so just always loved the game and just wanted to be involved in the game in some way."

She graduated from University of Tennessee-Martin in 1969 and quickly found work as the head coach of three sports—basketball, volleyball, and tennis—at Austin Peay State University. A column in *The* (Clarksville, Tennessee) *Leaf-Chronicle* titled "Gals Tennis Team Unbeaten at Peay" represents how much of a lift women's sports was at that time. "There's an undefeated athletic team on the Austin Peay State University campus. Austin Peay's tennis team. No, not boys—GIRLS! 'Seriously, we have a girls tennis team at Austin Peay,' said its coach Lin Dunn yesterday as he [sic] tried to convince us of the fact. 'And we have won three straight matches.'"

The tennis team finished 11–0, by the way. Dunn recalled more than a half-century later: "No scholarships, no budget, no support! Surprised we got to use the courts!"

Dunn did it all. She played summer softball with Pat Summitt before she was Pat Summitt. But basketball was her true love. Dunn's basketball coaching path included many stops along the way—Mississippi, Miami, Purdue, and the ABL's Portland Power. And then it was on to the WNBA, where she had the idea of pairing Lauren Jackson, a versatile big, in Seattle with a rookie point guard the Storm drafted named Sue Bird. It worked out okay—Seattle won titles with them in 2004 and 2010. Dunn headed to Indiana, where she coached the Tamika Catchings-led Fever to the 2009 WNBA Finals and won it all in 2012.

Dunn retired in 2014, but retirement isn't really how Lin Dunn does things, so she quickly pivoted to working on Matthew Mitchell's staff at Kentucky and advising the Fever before Indiana's difficulties building a team, following Catchings' own retirement from play after the 2016 season, called for a talent evaluator of the kind rarely seen in basketball history. Indiana drafted in the lottery each season between 2018 and 2021. Only Kelsey Mitchell, selected second overall in 2018, lived up to the billing of a lottery pick, while two of their four picks, Lauren Cox in 2020 and Kysre Gondreszick in 2021, failed to even stick in the league. "Nothing takes the place of experience," Dunn said. "And so all of the years of experience that I had evaluating talent in college, 26 years I think I was in college, and then another 20-plus years evaluating talent in the WNBA, it is just so valuable and just so beneficial. And so I think you're accurate that we were struggling with some free-agency situations, and we were struggling with some draft picks and that they just needed some help from someone with experience. And there's nothing that takes the place of experience. I give them all credit for saying, 'Hey, let's get some help from someone who's been there, done that, and has a history of evaluating talent.' And so that's exactly why I was willing to come in and help them."

What began as a part-time role consulting grew into the interim general manager role and, finally, the full-time gig on a three-year plan to turn the Fever back into contenders by 2024.

"What triggered me to come out of retirement and help the Fever was to see where they were at that particular time, that they were struggling, and that they needed some help and support," Dunn recalled. "And I was willing to do that because I had invested so many years of my career in them, and so when I saw that they needed some help, I was happy to do that. I don't think I realized when I first started doing it how fully invested I would become."

Over her half-century of evaluating talent, she'd come to an in-depth, comprehensive approach to determining player value in scouting. "I have a specific way that I go about evaluating players in particular for the draft," she said. "What I'm really looking at—a lot of research, a lot of time, a lot of effort goes into making a decision, and I use all the resources that I have. I use college coaches, I use college assistants, I use media; some of the women and men that broadcast the games year after year, they're in the press conferences, they're in the practices, they're in the shootarounds, and so they interact with these prospects as much or more than anybody. And so there I have a group of people, of resources, that I use to evaluate a player.

"And then I have a list of things related to size, speed, quickness, agility, adaptability, character. There's a lot that goes into making a decision about a player, and then I also have to be very objective in that I know college coaches are certainly not going to throw their player under the bus. And so I have to listen carefully to what they're saying and maybe read behind the lines if there is a minor issue. And I expect the college head coach to really take a positive position with their players. So that's why sometimes I would also talk to the assistants, talk to the trainer, might even talk to a past coach that had moved on, just trying to get as much information as I can about a player.

"How competitive are they? How hard do they work? Are they the first one at practice? Are they the last one to leave? How do they interact? I love watching how they interact on the bench with their teammates. How do they interact with their coaches? Because once we get players to the pros, I'm not going to really change their character.

I don't think I'm going to change their love of the game or I don't think I'm going to change their competitive spirit. So they better come with that, and I better evaluate that now. Can I teach them a drop step? Can I teach them a defensive crossover move that might help them grow their skills? Yeah, but there's some things about their character and who they are that are already ingrained. And so I'm really interested in their family, that dynamic, and just as much information as I could get before I make a decision. And so it's not done lightly."

So yes, while there were absolutely newcomers to women's basketball who confidently declared that Clark was unlike anyone they'd ever seen step on the court, it was the confidence in her ability from people like Dunn that truly reinforced the kind of impact she'd have on the court from the moment she entered the WNBA.

Dunn and the Fever took a similar approach to the one they'd utilized in 2023 after they received the top overall pick, knowing Aliyah Boston of South Carolina was the clear top option but allowing her the space to enjoy her senior season. "We let her do her college career," Dunn said.

The staff saw Clark play one game after securing the top pick, and that was it. "We did the same thing with Aliyah Boston. We did not want to be a distraction," Dunn said. "We did not want to be anything or do anything that was disruptive, be very respectful. We were available if her parents or if her agent wanted to contact us and had any questions, but we were trying to stay behind the scenes and let her enjoy and experience her final season."

By January of 2024, Clark reached the conclusion that it was time for the next chapter in her life. Dunn sat on her couch and reveled in the flood of text messages coming in. But Dunn wasn't excited in the sense of being surprised. In her mind it had all come together the moment the ping pong balls fell Indiana's way. Boston served as the good-luck charm at the lottery to produce a second-straight top pick. "I mean, she's smart, her family's smart, her coaches are smart," Dunn said. "They knew we had the best chances of winning the lottery. They knew we had the best chances of her being selected by us, and I think it was a perfect fit. I think she's the Big Ten. Indiana, Indianapolis, sits in the heart of the Big Ten. She's won Big Ten championships in Gainbridge Arena as a college player…she's a four- or five-hour drive home. So, absolutely, it was a perfect fit…. But I knew the minute we won the lottery pick in December. I'm thinking, *Okay, we won the lottery. Caitlin Clark's coming to the Fever. It's set.*

Still, Lisa Bluder and Jan Jensen hoped they'd get the chance to coach Clark for a fifth year—but only if it was what she wanted, too. They didn't want to strong-arm her.

"So we just pointed out both ways," Jensen recalled. "And, of course, we tried to get her to stay but in a really cool way, right? Not in a way like, 'Oh, that's going to be terrible' but pointing out that's going to be different. But I think that she needed to go…. Oh, you were a little disappointed, right? Just like when you're recruiting in some ways you're like, *Ah, you could have had one more*, but yet you understood it. And I think she'd grown and was ready, wanted to spread her wings."

She announced officially that she was making the next leap on Leap Day, February 29, before speaking to reporters about it the next day. "Going into Senior Night, having that decision clear, not only for myself, but our fans, my teammates, I think that was super important," said Clark, while still wearing her black Iowa practice jersey and looking more relaxed behind the podium than she had in a few weeks. "Honestly, just getting the weight of the world off my shoulders and being able to enjoy this last month with my teammates, I think, is the biggest thing. I think I kind of knew in my heart, honestly. I've gone honestly back and forth a little bit, especially early in the year. And I think as the season played out, it became more clear to me, and I know I said the beginning of the year, 'I will definitely feel [it] in my gut and know in my gut.' And I think that's exactly what happened. I knew what was going to be the right step for me…I'm ready for the next kind of chapter of my life, too. I think I've known for a little while, honestly, and I've had quite a few conversations with our coaching staff, and they were always very supportive in helping me try to understand both sides and see both sides. And I think especially over the last couple of weeks, my decision has become more clear."

Meanwhile, the Fever, immediately, experienced the kind of early data suggesting that the long struggle to transfer college allegiances to WNBA teams had ended with Clark's ascension. Both the winning of the lottery—before Clark had even declared for the draft—along with Clark's declaration itself drove a spike in season ticket sales for Indiana a month before the season. By the time she declared, Indiana's schedule had been released, and the prices for Clark games not only jumped at Gainbridge Fieldhouse for home games, but also everywhere she was scheduled to play, all before seeing her log a minute of WNBA court time. Ultimately, five of the 11 other teams would move at least one Fever game from their regular arenas to larger venues to accommodate demand and then would sell out those larger arenas, too. "We expected sold out, standing room-only for the first home game," Dunn said. "The wow moment for me was that it continued to happen every home game. And then the other thing that was—and I'll be real honest with you: it was a surprise to me—I did not anticipate that we would go to away arenas and they would be sold out. Now that was a surprise. I felt like we were really going to do something special at home based on our season ticket sales, etc., but I had no idea that this was going to happen on the road. That was probably, of all the things, that was probably the biggest surprise for me."

And for the WNBA, a particularly happy surprise. If the league had a chance to pick any moment in its history to drop the Caitlin Clark Effect into its business operations, commissioner Cathy Engelbert could not have scripted it any better. The league was riding an upswing in key performance indicators like ticket sales and television ratings. But with its current media rights deal set to end in 2025 and negotiations active for the next one, suddenly all of the numbers and expectations for both the viewership and the payday to correspond to it changed dramatically from incremental change to a sea change. "The main strategy, as you know, I've had since I came in, not having run a sports league before, were three things: household names, rivalries, and games of consequence," Engelbert said in March 2024 when asked whether Clark was impacting the then-ongoing media rights deal negotiations. "I've been talking about it since Caitlin's announcement on our social media accounts. It's the confluence of a lot of different things, but it's all anchored in that strategy around a household name—Caitlin being one. We have current players who are those as well, future players we're so fortunate to have in women's basketball. It's not just Caitlin. It's some of these other players like the Angel Reeses, the Paige Bueckers, the Cameron Brinks, the Rickea Jacksons, what a great couple years of classes, no matter which players come out or don't. And then behind them, JuJu Watkins and Hannah Hidalgo, and behind them will be the next generation of Caitlins.... So I'm really proud of the product on the court. But, yeah, that is all a confluence of this positive momentum that's going to help us in our next media deal negotiations and with our corporate partners. So, that's helpful, too."

A few weeks later, the WNBA ad campaign began running during the NCAA Tournament. Engelbert had stated a goal of $100 million a year for the new media rights deal back in 2022. By July of 2024, the WNBA had agreed to a new media rights deal with ESPN, NBC, and Amazon valued at $200 million a year, one which left some national game inventory over for additional potential deals that was expected to earn the WNBA a total of around $260 million per year over the next 11 years. The league's previous deal with ESPN paid out an annual fee of $33 million in 2025. That represented growth over previous years. The league's trajectory—even had Clark not declared for the draft—combined with a growing market for women's sports live game properties would have landed the WNBA more money per year in its next deal. The factor of eight came from the audience Clark brought to the league.

That excitement manifested itself even when Clark wasn't in uniform but merely adjacent to it. Mobs gathered around the Brooklyn Academy of Music (BAM) hoping for a glimpse of Clark as she entered the premises for the 2024 WNBA Draft. The league hadn't held the draft in a place that allowed for fans since 2016 when a relatively sparsely attended draft took place at Mohegan Sun Arena. In the intervening years, the WNBA held drafts in places like Spring Studios, a smaller venue than the Westchester County Center, along with Nike's New York headquarters and the second floor of an electronics store, Samsung 837. (It was possible to be heard without shouting from one end of that draft room to the other.)

A packed house at BAM, along with 2.45 million people—more than three times as many viewers as the 2023 draft, which itself had been 42 percent higher than the 2022 WNBA Draft television audience—provided additional evidence that the Clark fans had followed her from Iowa to Indiana. There'd be, of course, a lot more of that to come.

Hitting the orange carpet in an all-Prada outfit, Clark, the first WNBA or NBA player to be outfitted by the storied company, cited her family, teammates, and coaches who'd be on hand to keep her grounded for this moment she'd worked for her entire life. "I'm just excited, honestly. It almost doesn't feel real in a way," Clark said, as her eyes peeked out over her sunglasses. "I think it all comes so fast, especially from the end of this season, and then you've got to flip the page really fast to this and enjoy this and soak this in. But this is once in a lifetime, so you've got to enjoy it and do it right."

When the announcement came from Engelbert, Clark briefly closed her eyes, stood up, and soaked in the moment, hugging her brothers, Blake and Colin, then her father, Brent, and her mother, Anne, before walking to the podium to hold up a Fever jersey—along with Engelbert—emblazoned with the No. 1. (She received her 22 soon after.) Immediately after Clark spoke with ESPN's Holly Rowe, her head coach at Iowa, Bluder, walked up to her and gave her a long embrace. "So proud of you," she said in an emotional moment for both of them.

"I think the biggest thing is I vividly remember Coach Bluder coming and doing my home visit in my house during my recruiting," Clark said we spoke a few minutes later on the balmy April night. "The biggest thing is we talked about this moment. We dreamed of this moment, but she also believed I would be here, and she coached me really hard to get to this moment. There were a lot of ups and downs, a lot of ups and downs, and something I really appreciate about Coach Bluder is: no matter what awards or success or wins we ever had or I had, she never stopped coaching me. She never stopped holding me accountable. She always thought there were ways for me to get better. And she still thinks that, and I still think that, and that's one of the things I just love about her. First of all, she believed I would be here from the day I committed to her—even before that when I was in eighth grade—but also she pushed me really hard to make me as good as I am."

That night Clark explained that keeping her trademark equilibrium was harder than it had been most of her big public moments. After all, when she's about to play a big game, she can focus on the task at hand, concentrate on her shots as she warms up, find ways to get her teammates ready for the night as well. But the day to day? "I feel like it doesn't change a ton from how I lived my life over the course of the last year," said Clark in a nod to just how much attention she received as a collegiate player. "Sponsorships stay the same. The people around me, agents and whatnot, have been able to help me and guide me through the course of the last year. And I don't know if I would be in this moment if it wasn't for a lot of them. And my mom has done a lot, my dad has done a lot. In college I always said, 'My main focus is on basketball.' That's why I've had every other opportunity in my life is because the way I carry myself, the way I play the game, and going into my professional career, I plan to do the same exact thing."

Then, the trademark smile telegraphed a wry remark. "I don't have to do school anymore. That's pretty exciting," Clark said. "I do have to get my degree. I graduate on May 14. But other than that, you know, my 110 percent focus is on basketball. And when I do that really well and carry myself really well, everything kind of just takes care of itself."

Crystalized in that moment for Dunn was precisely why she didn't worry, even a little bit, about what it would take for Clark the person to succeed in a 2024 wilder and more pressure-packed than any year for any women's athlete since Billie Jean King. Even Simone Biles experienced those searing tests of character for short bursts during the Olympics. But an entire season at this level of brightness? Well, Clark could handle it. She's just proven that. And reflecting on it when it was all over, Dunn isn't sure anyone else could have done it. "I don't know any," Dunn said in October of 2024. "I haven't coached anybody that's ever experienced what she has experienced her last year in college or her rookie season in the pros. Not one that's had to deal with the challenges under the microscope and the visibility that she's had...I'm so impressed with how she handled it. She stays grounded. She's a Midwestern kid that likes to have fun and likes to laugh. And I love the fact that the season's over, and she's on the golf course hitting golf balls and trying to outdrive everybody. So it's that competitive spirit but having fun and enjoying what she's doing. So, no, she's definitely one of a kind."

After being selected No. 1 overall, she swapped out her Prada shoes for Uggs shortly after she finished talking to the media. And that night she celebrated first at Tao Nightclub, then at a private party in her honor at the Fleur Room in Chelsea. Every bit of her itinerary made its way into the *New York Post's* Page Six.

About an hour after Clark left the draft to begin her night, her Iowa teammates received a shocking, second announcement. At the 18th overall pick, the Las Vegas Aces selected Kate Martin, who had not been invited to the draft by the WNBA and simply happened to be in the audience to support Clark. She hugged Cedar Rapids' own Jaida Gyumri, then Gabbie Marshall (two fellow Hawkeyes), before turning and embracing her aunt and Dorcas Andersen's granddaughter, Jensen, just weeks from Jansen taking over the Iowa program from Bluder. "I was here to support Caitlin, but I was hoping to hear my name called," Martin said on the ESPN broadcast that night. "All I wanted was an opportunity and I got it. So, I'm really excited."

Gyumri and Marshall, standing a few feet away in the audience, had tears in their eyes. Martin wasn't supposed to reach the pros. This wasn't in the script. "I don't know if this has been a dream," Kate's father, Matt, told WQAD News that night. "I know playing Iowa women's basketball has been a dream for her…and I think she's reset her goals, and hopefully she can make the team, and we've got more basketball to watch."

Less than a month later, she earned that final roster spot in Las Vegas. She became the fan favorite in Las Vegas she'd been in Iowa and played significant minutes for a WNBA semifinalist as a rookie. At the Barclays Center ahead of Game Two of the WNBA semifinals against the New York Liberty in October, I asked her just how much her reality had exceeded her dreams. "I mean, it's crazy, honestly, surreal, right?" Martin responded. "I've talked about it before, but this entire year has been a whirlwind. And I feel super grateful to be here right now, and we've talked in the locker room. I've never competed for a WNBA championship before, but I've been blessed to compete for championships before at every level that I've played at, and so it's pretty cool that I'm getting to be a part of another playoff contention."

Evelyn Brehm said she and her teammates saw themselves in Martin, who grew up with Iowa basketball player posters on her ceiling. In 2024 Clark's jersey sold the most in the WNBA, reflecting her global stardom. But Martin, who came off the bench for the Aces, checked in at fourth in the entire league in jersey sales.

The Hornettes love Caitlin Clark. But they identify with Kate Martin. Why did Martin think that was the case? "Maybe because I played like them," Martin said. "I'm just a very fundamentally sound player. I'm not flashy. I'm not gonna go out and throw behind-the-back passes or get oohs and ahhs, but I'll knock down open threes, I'll make the right reads, and I'll play defense. So maybe that's what they mean by that. That's kind of how it was at Iowa, too. And what we were taught was, 'You've got to get the fundamentals down, and you have to play team basketball.' And that's what I love to do, and it's gotten me very far. Obviously, I'm in the WNBA. Who would have thought?" She smiled at the statement, as if still surprised by it. "I don't know. But here I am, and it's worked for me."

She impressed Aces assistant coach Natalie Nakase so much that when the expansion Golden State Valkyries hired her as their first ever head coach, Nakase successfully pushed for the Valkyries to select Martin in the expansion draft. Playing like the Hornettes in 1962 could win you a state title. Playing like the Hornettes in 2024 meant you could play basketball as your profession.

That's just what Clark got to do for the first time on May 14, 2024, when she took the floor for the Fever in the team's WNBA season opener against the Connecticut Sun in a sold-out Mohegan Sun Arena. As early evening fell on Uncasville, Connecticut, a chill in the air suggested far more of the Caitlin Clark Iowa March past than the Caitlin Clark Fever of the summer to come. But few in the town felt that chill. Uncasville is a true company town with few businesses outside of the 250,000-square foot Mohegan Sun Casino. For fans to reach the arena where the Sun play, it is necessary to enter and either walk past seemingly endless roulette tables and slot machines or journey through a massive indoor shopping mall, then take a sharp turn. But as she sat down and faced the questioning of reporters 80 minutes before she'd officially begin her WNBA career, Clark had a legion of fans and a sea of 22s (mostly of Iowa but more than a handful of the Clark jerseys which had sold out on Fanatics.com less than an hour after the Fever made the Clark pick official on WNBA draft night) visible as well, choking off the walking path in both directions.

Clark entered the building flanked by her new teammate, Katie Lou Samuelson, who'd been signed by the Fever as a supersized Martin to hit threes and guard multiple positions. She also brought with her the experience playing in front of massive crowds from her time starring in college at UConn, something Boston lived through as well during her tenure playing for Dawn Staley and South Carolina. Fever head coach Christie Sides noted this when asked pregame about the ways she prepared her group for this extra added attention. "When it's time to play basketball, Caitlin is locked in," Sides said while sitting at the podium in a back hallway at Mohegan Sun, as temporary chairs had been set up to accommodate assembled media. "She just has this crazy competitive spirit and she just wants to do whatever it takes to win. She was walking to the bus, she still has fun, tries to keep it light, but when it's time to go out, she is going to do whatever it takes for the Indiana Fever to have a chance to win this game."

Clark sat in the locker room, having quickly changed into her uniform, eager to get out onto the court. She finally emerged, looked up at the clock, and her first thought was of frustration—*Why hadn't the 90-minute countdown clock to gametime even begun?* The arrival time was earlier than she was used to at Iowa. It was one of many adjustments that came with the pro game. The entire experience was an exercise in hurry up and wait for Clark, who battled within herself the emotions of knowing she'd never have another first WNBA game, not only eagerly wanting to have that experience, but also wanting to put it behind her and learn from it. "I feel like a little kid," Clark said, but looking anything like one as a seeming veteran of the press conference because, of course, she was. "I just feel really excited more than anything. I don't really get nervous, I don't get anxious, I just get a giddy excitement, feeling like I just can't wait for the moment to be here and just go out there and play the game and have a lot of fun.... If we walk away without a win tonight, and we know we did everything right to get better, you have a quick turnaround, you get to play again on Thursday. That's what this league is. You can't just dwell on one loss. Obviously, our goal is to go out there and win and dominate in all areas, but I think our group knows if we go out there and play the way we should for 40 minutes, we're going to get the result we want, but we're also going to get a lot better."

The familiarity even extended to the opposing coach, Stephanie White, who had been a Big Ten icon in her own right at Purdue, leading the Boilermakers to the 1999 NCAA title, and was royalty in the state of Indiana that Clark now called home. She even announced Big Ten games during the WNBA offseason. She'd served on Dunn's staff with the Fever, then succeeded her as head coach back in 2014 before moving to Vanderbilt, then to the Sun, where she entered her second season as head coach in 2024. "She's always been somebody that's been supportive of my game, and it's been fun to talk to her at shootarounds throughout my college career and always been really supportive," Clark said of White. "So I think the biggest thing is [that] it's fun to get up to go against her now, for my first time, after her calling a lot of my games. Now I get to play against her. So I think that's gonna be a lot of fun for the both of us."

Truthfully, the night was a lot more fun for White than Clark in ways that circumstances almost guaranteed. Clark's Fever were at anything but full capacity. In the backcourt Mitchell, the Ohio State star and long-tenured Indiana shooting guard, was a perfect complement to Clark in every way. But Mitchell had been slowed by an ankle injury during the preseason, playing that night in what was a gametime decision by the Fever training staff but coming off the bench for just 17 minutes. Instead, veteran Erica Wheeler, herself more of a point guard than a perimeter threat, started next to Clark, and her lack of shooting prowess from three allowed the Sun to spend less time focused on her and concentrate more of their defensive pressure on Clark herself.

Much of that pressure came from DiJonai Carrington, the woman who drew Clark as her primary defensive assignment for the opener. One of the best examples of how the WNBA was not, as of 2024, large enough to accommodate all of its talent, Carrington excelled for Tara VanDerveer's Stanford Cardinal for four years, punctuating her collegiate career with a standout post-grad year at Baylor. But drafted

20th overall, she struggled early in her career to earn regular minutes with the Sun under Curt Miller before breaking through as White's first weapon off the bench in 2023. In 2024 she'd earn WNBA All-Defensive First Team honors. At 5'11" with long arms and a remarkable ability to anticipate where an offensive player was headed and get there first, she was a human manifestation of the welcome-to-the-WNBA moment. And when Carrington was out of the game or the Fever scheme engineered a switch, it produced anything but a breather for Clark. Built like a freight train and famous for her physicality, the 6'2", 203-pound Alyssa Thomas is the most versatile defender in the entire league.

Fans across Mohegan Sun Arena rose to their feet. Clark looked down at her feet, took a deep breath. Thomas kept on talking quietly with a playful smile on her face. And then came the tip right into the hands of Clark. Carrington gave her absolutely no space, but Clark bounced a pass through a pick set by Boston to her fellow No. 1 pick, who took advantage of the single coverage from Brionna Jones to finish at the rim. Assist No. 1 of 337 for Clark was in the books. That assist-to-bucket combination, which logged its first connection, would come to define Indiana's 2024 season.

Very little else came easily that night for Clark and the Fever, though, as Carrington had forecast to us the day before. "I mean, 7:00 tomorrow, you'll see," Carrington told reporters. "At the end of the day, they have to guard us just as much as we have to guard them, and I think that that wear and tear, that physicality of running her off ball screens or just being physical with her on both ends of the floor, it wears people down defensively. We scout, we take away the things that people like to do, and she's going to score. She's a really good player, and she's gonna get to her spots a couple times, but we have to limit those."

True to form, WNBA officiating helped limit Clark's flow and exposure to a national television audience by calling her for a pair of fouls on Thomas with contact entirely imperceptible to the naked eye, forcing her to the bench. Clark found a better rhythm in the second half and cut the Sun lead to six midway through the third quarter. "I would say definitely in the second half I just felt we ran stuff a little bit better," a clearly fatigued Clark said following the game from the podium. Dressed in casual white warmups, she rested her chin on her left hand. "We got into some more actions. We swung the ball a little bit better. I think I was able to get a few mismatches and capitalize on those opportunities."

But the Sun, fresh off a 27–13 season, never relented on the Fever or Clark for the rest of the game, winning 92–71. Clark finished with 20 points, but it took 15 shots to get there, and she turned the ball over 10 times in her pro debut. Carrington dribbled out the final seconds, her right hand elevated, asking for the Sun crowd to get louder before striding over to Thomas, who'd logged a triple-double—commonplace for A.T., rare for anyone else—and placing a virtual crown on her head. Just like any other game, they'd all insisted. Not exactly.

The Sun entered the postgame press conference giddy. Carrington was flanked on the podium by Thomas and DeWanna Bonner, the 15-year veteran who was fifth all time in the WNBA in scoring. White had pointed out pregame that Bonner had spent a career deserving the national television audience and sellout crowd at Mohegan Sun Arena—the first since 2003 in the franchise's very first game—she experienced that night.

Bonner and Thomas had an easy rapport, and no wonder—the two were engaged to be married. A reporter asked them both who would like to talk about Carrington, and then a quick rock-paper-scissors game right behind Carrington produced A.T. as the winner, and Thomas happily spoke about her younger teammate. "Nai's huge," Thomas said. "We knew what she was capable of. This is what we expect from her, but to take on that job and to play it at that high level and do things on both ends, we're proud of her." She paused a beat and looked at Carrington. "But don't get too big-headed."

Once again, the nuance of the moment could have been so easily lost. Carrington's 2024 encapsulated this as well as anyone's. Long before Clark even matriculated at the University of Iowa, Carrington's calling card was tough, physical perimeter defense. She spent years honing those skills at two of the most elite colleges in the country, then four years with the Sun. And just as she reached the starting lineup, Carrington got bombarded with questions—not just when the Fever came to play but almost every media availability—about Clark. She answered questions like a pro, too, but the faint annoyance was visible on her face as she heard and processed that she was about to be asked another in the variation of Clark questions all season—usually from a reporter just doing their job after finally getting an editor to assign a women's basketball story to satisfy readers who wanted to know what this Clark business was all about. It was the same flash of annoyance Clark would sometimes show when the 1,000th version of a question was posed to her.

Instead, somehow, the story kept getting told as if that attention and the financial windfall that came with Clark were somehow mutually exclusive, that players could be expected to either feel entirely grateful that Clark's ascension to the league had supercharged growth or, as the best basketball players on the planet, they'd worked relentlessly to beat her no differently than they'd attack any other star player, especially a rookie with so much to learn. Perhaps the discourse did not hold room for this dichotomy. But for dozens of WNBA players I spoke to about this, both dynamics were at play. So was it difficult for Carrington to effusively praise Clark even as she fulfilled the obligations of her job to battle her fiercely on the court? Of course. Why was that even her responsibility?

As for Clark: her stardom carried with it the toxic mix of fandom, social media, and the curdled American conversation about race and gender in America simply because every single part of American life does. That is inescapable. It was particularly so in a presidential election year ultimately waged between one of the most open racists in recent American life and a woman of color.

Fandom is inherently irrational to begin with. The substantial number of Clark fans, whose exuberance failed to properly contextualize her within the proud history of the WNBA, was to be expected, too. That there were forces in American life who saw Clark as an opportunity to attack Black women using her name, image, and likeness was as disturbing as it was predictable. Harnessing those forces has proven impossible for the largest institutions in American life. The Democratic Party and its allies spent more than one billion dollars trying to do just that in the 2024 presidential election. But somehow many people seemed to expect Clark to control these dark forces with a simple wave of a magic wand or a sustained public effort amid the work trying to prove herself in the most challenging basketball league in the world.

Amid Clark's 2024 season of greatness on the court and fundamental reset of financial and audience expectations for women's basketball off of it, this undercurrent would get louder, more pronounced. Meanwhile 2.1 million people watched on ESPN2, while on ESPN, available in more households, the NHL playoffs drew an audience of 1.9 million people. The prioritizing of the NHL over the WNBA was a product of the previous media rights deals. Clark was changing the pecking order of sports in America in real time.

That is not to suggest that the on-court battles would get any easier. Just as WNBA officials routinely provided fresh evidence that the league had not conspired on Clark's behalf on the court, the same proved true with Clark's early-season schedule, a three-week-long welcome-to-the-NBA moment in travel form. Following the opener on May 14, the Fever faced the Liberty—not in nearby New York but back home in Indianapolis. Two days later, they faced the Liberty again on May 18, but this time in New York. And two days after that, they took on the Sun on May 20—back home in Indiana.

Incidentally, while Connecticut was a difficult opponent, perhaps the only perimeter defender who could challenge Carrington for best in the league played for the Liberty: Betnijah Laney. So that was four games, eight days, and the two most difficult matchups for Clark in the league to begin her career. New York, incidentally, reached the WNBA Finals in 2023 and won it all in 2024, featuring multiple MVPs in its starting lineup in Breanna Stewart and Jonquel Jones, along with a guard in Sabrina Ionescu, who was selected first overall in 2020 and had her best season yet in 2024. "This is the professional league," Mitchell said after the second New York game, a 91–80 loss that dropped Indiana to 0–3. Clark scored 22, added eight assists, and six rebounds but turned the ball over eight times as well. "I don't know what people expect or what they're looking for, but this is going to take a little time. And I think that with us and what we're trying to build, it's only right that we kind of take these moments and utilize them. Us battling against the best of the best, it's only how we're going to get better, right? So, in the trenches with Stewie and you go play A.T. and DeWanna Bonner, I mean, those guys are the best, right? So if we can compete and show early, how we can get better down the stretch [so] at the end we can be in the playoff run."

Indiana's reward for that gauntlet was…a West Coast trip, beginning with the contenders in Seattle on May 22 on to Los Angeles on May 24 to face the Sparks, one of only two games in Indiana's first 11 that wasn't against a top five team in the league, followed by finishing a back-to-back in Las Vegas to take on the defending champion Aces on May 25, then back home for the Sparks on May 28, the Storm on May 30, the Chicago Sky on June 1, capped off by a flight to New York, and a third game against the Liberty on the road June 2. That made for 11 games in 20 days. It was a gauntlet scheduled before Clark had even declared for the draft or the Fever had won the lottery. No conspiracy here, just a stretch as difficult as any experienced by a WNBA team, dating back over two decades, and at the very start of the season and the very beginning of Clark's career.

And by the time the Fever arrived in New York, they were also navigating yet another distraction, one that brought out the very worst elements of the entire 2024 Caitlin Clark discourse. The Sky were—in so many ways both justified and sad—the foil for the Fever. The Sky's most famous player was Reese, a rookie with an enormous following and a huge basketball upside as well. She became a go-to talking point for everyone who wished to counter the inarguable fact of Clark's effect on audience and interest in the league, a construct that tried to force the retrograde idea that there must be credit given to every author of this victory for women's basketball in 2024—or even stranger that the win belonged to everyone except the demonstrated reason for the largest growth.

Regardless, it did Reese a disservice that in a year she emerged as the league's best rebounder while increasing Chicago Sky home attendance 21 percent, the formulation of how she was evaluated so often in the public discourse either dismissed those accomplishments by comparing them to Clark or in weird, bad-faith ways pretended they were somehow the same or more significant than what Clark was doing. That was already happening with the added ingredient of the LSU–Iowa games in two of the highest-profile performances of Reese and Clark's college careers, when their two pro teams faced off for the first time on June 1 in a Saturday afternoon, nationally televised game that would draw 1.53 million pairs of eyeballs.

The game was living up to its advanced billing when Sky guard Chennedy Carter drained a jump shot from 10 feet out to cut Indiana's lead to 53–49. As Boston then prepared to inbound the ball to Clark, who didn't have it yet, Carter walked straight at her, called her a "Bitch," and then knocked her to the ground before walking away.

Incredibly, Carter was initially charged with only a common, away-from-the-ball foul. The Fever rightly felt as if Clark had not been protected by the officials in that moment. The Sky, a franchise which had worked through the years to alienate any local reporters who even attempted to cover them and never missed an opportunity to maximize a public-relations disaster, didn't make Reese available to reporters after the game, while Carter, asked about the play and given a chance to provide her side of the story, simply said, "Next question" and went on to declare, "I ain't answering no Caitlin Clark questions."

Clark, even in the minutes following the game, took the high road. "I wasn't expecting it," Clark said. "It is what it is. It's a physical game. Go make the free throw and execute on offense, and I feel like that's kind of what we did."

The next day, I asked Fever Coach Sides what we learned about Clark in that moment. "She showed [who she is] last night when she just got up and we just kept playing," Sides said, her voice all but gone from the end of the 20-day gauntlet. "I mean, all she did was ask the officials to review it, and she said they didn't really want to [do that], but I really applaud her for how she handled it last night."

On the Chicago side, on Monday, 48 hours after the game, the Sky put out a statement from Teresa Weatherspoon, the team's head coach. "Physical play, intensity, and a competitive spirit are hallmarks of Chicago Sky basketball. Chennedy got caught up in the heat of the moment in an effort to win the game," the statement read. "She and I have discussed what happened and that it was not appropriate, nor is it what we do or who we are. Chennedy understands that there are better ways to handle situations on the court, and she will learn from this, as we all will."

Forty-eight hours in the 2024 media environment might as well be a year. The league upgraded the foul to a flagrant one, fined the Sky and Reese, who hadn't done anything wrong and wasn't even on the floor for the flagrant foul moment, for failing to be available postgame. But all the ammunition needed for those who were looking for a chance to scapegoat every single WNBA player, particular Black players and specifically Reese, had arrived.

At the Monday practice, Carter finally addressed the incident…sort of. "I'm a competitor, and I'm going to com-pete no matter who you are and no matter who's in front of me. So that's just what it was," Carter said. "Heat-of-the-moment-play, we're getting at it. We're getting back and forth. It's basketball. It's all hoops. After we finish the game, it's all love." She added, "I'm seeing a lot of things—players, fans not understanding who I am as a player. You have to understand me as a person, too, and don't just look at one tape and form an opinion about me. I'm truly a passionate

The Hornettes gather in Van Horne, Iowa, for their annual reunion. From left to right in the front row: Marj (Dutton) Stephenson, Evelyn (Brehm) Wiebke, Jean (Garbers) Kubu, and Mickey Schallau. Back row is: Marla (Heitman) McBride, JoAnn (Heitman) Schallau, and coach Larry Wiebke. *(Evelyn Brehm)*

You cannot drive through Moravia, population 626 as of 2023, without seeing Molly Kazmer on the town mural right next to the post office on the downtown square. *(Molly Kazmer)*

Molly Kazmer and Caitlin Clark chat following an event in Kansas City in February 2025. *(Legends of the Ball, Inc.)*

Molly Kazmer, who starred in the first women's professional basketball league in the United States, remains a pioneering figure in women's sports, and her visionary ideas drive innovation to this day. *(Molly Kazmer)*

Molly Kazmer hangs out with Brent and Anne Nizzi-Clark, the parents of Caitlin Clark, at the 2024 All-Star Game in Phoenix. *(Molly Kazmer)*

Iowa high school legends Connie Kunz, Molly Bolin, Denise Long, and Joan Uhl shoot hoops. *(Molly Kazmer)*

The granddaughter of Dorcas Andersen, current Iowa head coach Jan Jensen was also a Iowa high school basketball star and has the hardware to prove it. *(Jan Jensen)*

Rutgers coach C. Vivian Stringer, who coached at Iowa from 1983 to 1995, hugs Iowa coach Lisa Bluder before their 2005 game in Iowa City. Rutgers assistant coach Jolette Law, who played at Iowa, is on the left. *(AP Images)*

Iowa head coach Lisa Bluder and associate head coach Jan Jensen try to restrain Caitlin Clark from talking to the referees during Nebraska's 82–79 win against Iowa in 2024. *(AP Images)*

Iowa head coach Lisa Bluder hugs Caitlin Clark during Senior Day in 2024. *(AP Images)*

Iowa's Caitlin Clark defends UConn's Paige Bueckers during the Sweet 16 round of the 2021 NCAA tournament. UConn won 92–72 as Bueckers had 18 points, nine rebounds, and eight assists, while Clark had 21 points and five assists. *(AP Images)*

Caitlin Clark shoots a three-point basket over UConn guard Ashlynn Shade as Iowa gets its revenge against UConn, defeating the Huskies 71–69 in the 2024 Final Four. *(AP Images)*

LSU's Angel Reese taunts Iowa's Caitlin Clark during LSU's 102–85 win in the 2023 national championship. *(AP Images)*

LSU guard Flau'jae Johnson defends Caitlin Clark, who gets revenge against LSU by leading Iowa to a 94–87 victory against the Tigers in the 2024 Elite Eight. *(AP Images)*

Caitlin Clark poses for a photo with WNBA commissioner Cathy Engelbert after being selected first overall by the Indiana Fever during the 2024 WNBA Draft. *(AP Images)*

Caitlin Clark and Angel Reese renew their rivalry in the WNBA. *(AP Images)*

person about the game, and I'm genuine. You can ask all my teammates. They've gotten to know me. They know the real Chennedy Carter. So I'm just saying, 'Don't form an opinion off of one little clip and you didn't even see the whole game and/or the play that led to that.'"

The problem for Carter is that the more context one uses, the harder it is to see her actions as rational—just as it creates a massive problem for those using Carter as an avatar for the supposed singular negative attitude from WNBA players as a whole toward Clark. Carter is one of the most talented players of her generation, a McDonald's All-American who enchanted everyone who had the opportunity to watch her during her collegiate career at Texas A&M. Nobody can get to the basket and finish as a guard quite as impressively as Carter. The projectability of her came from the idea that if she added a consistent three-point shot and got her teammates involved regularly, she'd be an unstoppable prototype combo guard.

The Atlanta Dream selected her fourth overall in the 2020 WNBA Draft just after Indiana, in need of a point guard, selected Cox instead. This didn't work out for a variety of reasons for the Fever, but the Dream, who simply couldn't pass up that much talent at the fourth spot, quickly learned why she'd fallen to fourth as well. According to The Next, Carter instigated multiple altercations with teammates, including Courtney Williams, a respected veteran now playing for the Minnesota Lynx. The Dream suspended her July 6, 2021, and sent her to the Sparks that winter. The Sparks benched her for poor conduct in 2022, waived her after one season, and she did not play in the WNBA in 2023.

The Sky signed her in 2024, and her production was undeniable. But multiple sources familiar with the locker room dynamic in Chicago told me that Weatherspoon had essentially created a lack of any rules or framework for both Carter and Reese, leading to a split in the team between those two players with Weatherspoon on one side and the rest of the roster on the other side. The team began the season 9–12 but finished 4–15, missing the playoffs. At the end of the 2024 season, Weatherspoon was fired by the Sky. The Sky announced a few weeks later that they would not be retaining Carter for the 2025 season.

That's a lot for Carter to fit in—all before her 26th birthday. None of it speaks well to her decision-making skills, her impulse control, or the likelihood this was a one-off fundamentally different from who she has been since entering the league. But it also reinforces just how embarrassing it was to numerous WNBA players I spoke to about this on background, particularly Black players with a wide range of feelings about both the Caitlin Clark Effect and the way the league was being covered. Being lumped in with Carter, of all players, as some kind of spokesperson for veterans in the league did not sit well.

But the subsequent uproar also further sowed deep mistrust from many players, especially when the loudest media voices were not from those who had typically covered the league at all. For instance, the editorial board of the Sky's hometown paper, the *Chicago Tribune*, wrote this: "The foul committed by Chicago Sky guard Chennedy Carter was egregious. Outside of a sporting contest, it would have been seen as an assault. Even within a sporting context, it was bad: before the ball even was inbounded, Carter came up from behind Clark, shoving her at the hip and knocking her over. Lip readers simultaneously construed a five-letter epithet dancing on the Sky player's lips. She should have been ejected from the game."

And it had real-world consequences for Carter's teammates. As Sky forward Brianna Turner explained later that week: "I've been called every racial slur imaginable lately, and my teammates have had it even worse."

If the *Tribune* editorial board had weighed in on any of the other foul calls in WNBA history—and plenty of them have been questionable—there is no public record of it. All of which to say is: a flammable situation grew that much worse.

And to think: that was just the first night of Clark's back-to-back games. By the time she arrived in New York for Game 11 in 20 days—it was only Game No. 9 for the Liberty, they hadn't played the day before, and were a veteran-laden team on its way to a 32–8 regular–season record—Clark was tired. But she understood already how to contextualize the moment for herself when I asked her how she felt about it. "Honestly, it makes me think back to college," said Clark that night just before taking on the Liberty. "My first couple years in college, I was still pretty frail—I still am pretty frail, but I feel like I added quite a bit of muscle in my college career. And so that was the tactic early on in my college career, too, is just be really physical with her because she's not probably as strong as everybody else, and usually I was a little bit faster than everybody else, so usually speed is what I try to use. So it reminds me of my early college career, and my strength will evolve over the course of having an offseason and having time to do those things, to focus on those things…. But also I grew up playing basketball with the boys, so it's always been physical and feisty, and that is what it is. You've got to find a way to hold your own. So it kind of reminds me of that, and then I grew up with two brothers. Things were very, very physical, a lot of blood, a lot of tears, so I'm definitely prepared for it."

There'd be no public feeling sorry for herself. And the message she'd send, every single time she got knocked down and got back up was clear: opponents can be as physical as they could get away with. It wasn't going to slow Clark down. The Fever lost that night 104–68. But with the loss, which dropped Indiana to 2–9, came the most precious commodity of all. I asked Clark's teammate, forward NaLyssa Smith, what she planned to do the following day. She answered without hesitation: "Sleep in!"

Despite all of these barriers to success, Clark was well on her way to one of the best statistical rookie seasons in the history of the WNBA. "What was interesting with Caitlin was watching her adapt and adjust what she was seeing by the opponents every game, even during the game," Dunn said in October 2024. "And that goes back to her basketball IQ and how intelligent she is, understanding, *So I'm getting the best defender, I'm getting the traps*, and so how to handle them, how to adjust to them. And so I give her a lot of credit because as it went along, the tougher the defenders got, the better she got because they made her better."

In her first 11 games, she was shooting 46.2 percent from two-point range, 29.7 percent from three, hitting 89.4 percent of her free throws—solid numbers but nothing extraordinary. The assists checked in at 6.4 per game, but the turnovers were too high: 5.4 per game. Still, compare her to WNBA rookies, and her supremacy even in this trying early period becomes clear. Clark's 70 total assists ranked her second among any WNBA player ever in her first 11 games behind only Suzie McConnell Serio's 78 for the 1998 Cleveland Rockers. Clark scored 172 points in those 11 games, which not only is far ahead of McConnell Serio's 100, but also is higher than any of the top 18 on that assist list.

The most comparable first 11 games involving both scoring and distributing came from Bird, who had 55 assists in her first 11 games but almost as many points as Clark with 170. She was significantly less efficient from two, making 39 percent, though she did hit 36.4 percent of her threes and 94.7 percent from the line. The mix made for a comparable true shooting percentage of 54.7 percent, while Clark checked in at 52.4 percent. "Let's go back to when Sue Bird came into the league," Dunn said. "We didn't have the talent then—that's 25 years ago, don't forget—that we have now. You look at the people. Carrington is all over her. Betnijah Laney is all over her. They're in traffic with her with post players that are as mobile and agile as guards now. So Sue really didn't have as much talent pushing her. I thought what happened for Caitlin is those defensive schemes early on that were tough, they were physical, they were tough, and they were constantly changing. She had to grow her ability to adapt and adjust and she did an excellent job, but she had to go through that. She had to experience that. And so I give those teams credit for helping make us better."

That said, absolutely everything about the loudest parts of the public discourse concerning Clark and USA Basketball's decision to leave her off the team got it wrong. Everything. The two sides settled on the extremes, as so often happens in sports public discourse. Either it was patently obvious that Clark belonged on the Olympic team, or there was no possible way USA Basketball should have even considered sending her to Paris 2024. The reality is: she was effectively the first alternate, and there was a compelling case to take her or to leave her off. Or as Clark put it: "A point everybody was making was like, 'Who are you taking off the team?'" Clark says. "And that was a tremendous point."

The guards, who, roughly speaking, would have been competing for the same spot as Clark, were: Kelsey Plum, Ionescu, Chelsea Gray, and Diana Taurasi. You could argue Jewell Loyd and Jackie Young were guards, too, but they both brought additional defensive versatility. So who is the one of the four you'd leave off the team? Plum and Gray were the two dominant forces behind consecutive WNBA championships for the Aces. Ionescu had leveled up and was in the process of leading the Liberty to the 2024 WNBA title.

Taurasi had the wisdom while competing for an incredible sixth gold medal.

It was certainly arguable that Clark was a more effective choice than Gray, who was still returning to form from her late-season injury in 2023. And Clark was performing at a higher level than Taurasi in part because she was 20 years younger. (If Clark plays for the 2044 Olympic team, Taurasi will be 62.) It all came down to the selection committee: Atlanta general manager Dan Padover, Sun president Jen Rizzotti, Staley, WNBA executive Bethany Donaphin, and former WNBA greats Seimone Augustus and DeLisha Milton-Jones. So naturally, when the decision came, much of the public pushback centered around USA Basketball head coach Cheryl Reeve, who not only doesn't have final say over the team, but also isn't even part of the deliberations. "USA Basketball's snub of Caitlin Clark was the worst player selection decision I've seen in my 40 years covering the Olympics. What a mistake!" journalist Christine Brennan wrote.

Much of Brennan's critique of the decision came not from the on-court play. Instead she argued that having Clark on the team would have given the USA Basketball women's team more attention. And though that probably is true—see also every single other example of Clark's basketball life and much of her non-basketball pursuits—not only was USA

Basketball firm about not using that as a consideration in the decision-making process, but also Clark herself did not want a spot on the team under those circumstances, though she was disappointed not to make the team. "I don't want to be there because I'm somebody that can bring attention," Clark told *Time* magazine in December 2024. "I love that for the game of women's basketball. But at the same time, I want to be there because they think I'm good enough. I don't want to be some little person that is kind of dragged around for people to cheer about and only watch because I'm sitting on the bench. That whole narrative kind of upset me because that is not fair. It's disrespectful to the people that were on the team, that had earned it, and were really good. And it's also disrespectful to myself."

Instead, the best possible thing happened for Clark and the Fever. She had extra motivation for the remainder of her season and immediately took her game to another level. Of course, that was likely happening soon regardless, as the Fever stopped playing 11 games every 20 days. Dunn saw it in every practice once the Fever actually had enough time off between games to even hold practices. But the results, whether spite-based or rest-based, are undeniable. In the games leading up to the Olympic snub, Clark shot 37.3 percent from the floor, averaged 16.3 points and six assists per game. After the announcement she shot 43.5 percent from the floor and averaged 20.6 points and 9.6 assists per game. Only Courtney Vandersloot, in the shortened 2020 season, averaged more than 9.6 assists per game in a full WNBA season. The mistakes came less and less as well. Her assist to turnover ratio was 59/51 in May. It was 79/61 in 11 June games. In six July games before the All-Star break, it was 75/33.

The Fever, too, started winning. Clark and Boston became lethal in the pick-and-roll. It was a new role for Boston, a new connection for them both. "With the way I got trapped, especially early in the season offensively, I think just getting better, me and A.B. together working out of that, I think you can tell the more we've played together, the better we've got in pick-and-roll situations," Clark told reporters gathered in Minnesota after she led the Fever to an 81–74 win on the same court she saw her first live WNBA game back in 2015. But it was the players around Clark, too.

Mitchell, now healthy, became the legitimate third part of the Big Three that Dunn had envisioned. Lexie Hull, given the gift of Clark passes and the freedom to play extended minutes and find her rhythm, turned into a WNBA Gabbie Marshall for the Fever offense, ultimately hitting 47.1 percent from deep while playing her trademark relentless defense, which freed up Clark and Mitchell to do more on the offensive end. Temi Fagbenle was a revelation as a big off the bench, providing support for Boston and Smith. Indiana won four straight in mid-June to re-enter the playoff mix. In an eight-day span from July 6–14, the Fever beat both WNBA finalists, New York and Minnesota. Then it was on to Phoenix, where the All-Stars, who weren't on the Olympic team, defeated the USA Basketball team 117–109. Clark, the leading vote-getter, had 10 assists, playing alongside the second-leading player in votes, her teammate, Boston.

And then she had a month of rest, practice, time in the gym, a chance to process everything that had happened with more of an offseason in season than she'd even experienced following the end of her senior year. A week after the Final Four, she'd been at the 2024 WNBA Draft. A week after that, she had training camp and went straight into her season. The rest was an absolute luxury. "I definitely feel more fresh and prepared," said Clark a little over an hour before returning to the court to take on the Phoenix Mercury on August 16. "Still understanding that this league is very difficult and getting back into the routine of things, I felt like we were playing good basketball right before the break and, especially myself, I felt like I was starting to get in the groove. So it was kind of a weird thing. I wanted to kind of keep playing. I felt like we were starting to find our flow together…and then you go on a month-long break, and it's like, 'Ah, you don't get to play for a month.' So I think there's definitely a balance on it. And I feel like we've been itching to get back out on the court, especially the last week. It's like we've been ready for it, and now you guys get to come out and show the work that you've put in."

Clark did that and more, scoring 29, dishing 10 assists, and the Fever simply overpowered a Mercury team which began 2024 with championship aspirations, 98–89. Notably, over the final 14 games, only the Fever and Lynx had identical offensive ratings of 109.6, which tied for best in the league. The critical distinction between the two? Indiana's defense improved over the start of the year, but that was still only good for 10th in the WNBA over the final 14 games. The Fever allowed 106.5 points per 100 possessions—ahead of only the non-playoff teams Dallas and Chicago. The leaders in defensive net rating in the final 14—the Sun—allowed 92.8 per 100 per possessions.

And the slow start meant that while the Fever were playing as well as anyone in the league, they still earned the six seed, meaning a first-round matchup against the three seed: the Sun and their lockdown defense. And the setup of the WNBA's playoff format meant that to even earn a home game in the playoffs, Indiana would need to win at least one of the first two games at Mohegan Sun to force a decisive Game Three back at Gainbridge Fieldhouse.

In Game One, an overwhelming 93–69 Sun victory, the final Caitlin contretemps of the season took place. In the first quarter, Carrington came over to close out on a Clark jump-pass. While coming down she poked Clark in the eye. The next day Brennan asked Carrington if it had been intentional. By that time players, coaches, and even other media members around the league had heard Brennan say and do things that called her objectivity into question. That frustration Carrington sometimes flashed earlier in the year? She didn't bother to hide it. "I don't even know why I would intend to hit anybody in the eye," Carrington responded in a clip that Brennan subsequently posted on social media. "That doesn't even make sense to me. But, no, I didn't. I didn't know I hit her actually. I was trying to make a play on the ball and I guess I followed through and I hit her. Obviously, it's never intentional. That's not even the type of player that I am."

Someone who has covered Carrington dating back to her collegiate days would have known that statement is true. Carrington is not Carter. But that understanding was missing here. Brennan's follow-up question then asked whether a celebration she and teammate Marina Mabrey had in the fourth quarter of the same game after Carrington sank a three-pointer—a clearly identifiable three-to-the-dome popularized by Carmelo Anthony after he made shots beyond the arc—was celebrating Carrington's poke of Clark's eye. Implicit in the question was Brennon not accepting Carrington's initial answer. "No, I just told you," Carrington said, "I didn't even know I hit her. So I can't laugh about something I didn't even know happened."

As always around Clark, everybody lost their collective minds. The level of abuse Carrington and other Sun players faced for the remainder of the series led Thomas—hardly one to complain—to say postgame following Game Two, "In my 11-year career, I've never experienced the racial comments from the Indiana Fever fanbase. It's unacceptable honestly," Thomas said. "There's no place for it. We've been professional throughout the whole entire thing, but I've never been called the things that I've been called on social media."

Thomas has played for more than a decade in the WNBA and has deserved every bit of the extra positive attention that's come with doing so in 2024. But though this is the WNBA, it is still in America. And the end of the WNBA as a safe space after being ignored by much of the rest of the culture comes with treatment from some people that no one—particularly not Thomas—deserves.

The WNBA Players' Association issued a scathing statement about Brennan, calling for her credential to be revoked for future events, which only served to amplify the issue further.

Brennan repeatedly refused to acknowledge any potential danger in throwing around accusations like this, claiming with some justification that reporters need to be able to ask difficult questions and that done responsibly such questions can allow players to destroy incorrect claims that can otherwise percolate on social media. But that requires a fuller understanding of the context. It requires a building of trust between reporter and interviewee and ignores the toxic work being done by too many.

Somehow, yet again, the only person whose instruments didn't stop working during this part of the flight was Clark, who laughed at a reporter asking whether or not Carrington's poke was intentional. "It wasn't intentional by any means," Clark said of the poke, laughing. "Just watch the play."

Clark was transcendent in Game Two with 25 points, six rebounds, and nine assists, but it wasn't enough. When that final buzzer sounded after an 87–81 Sun win, Clark and the Fever gathered for an impromptu huddle. Erica Wheeler, who spent 2024 as a veteran on hand to help Clark navigate it all, asked her if she was okay. Clark nodded, but Wheeler kept her arm around Clark's shoulders, hand on her head, making it clear she had her teammate's back—in this case literally. "That's a good little taste of what's possible for this organization," said Clark, sitting and processing it just minutes after her season ended. "There's a lot to hold our heads up high about. This is a team that won five games two years ago. So we're a young group, pretty inexperienced group, but we came together as a group and had a lot of fun together."

Only at the very end did her voice break at all. She was very much herself in this difficult moment—by turns serious and analytical, funny, and not afraid to poke fun at herself. As the press conference came to a close, Clark was asked to grade herself. "I don't know how I'd grade myself. I'm a tough grader," the former honor student at Dowling Catholic said. "The fun part is I feel like I'm just scratching the surface. I'm one that's nitpicking every little thing I do, and I know I want to help this franchise get even better, help my teammates get better, be better for my teammates and I know there's a lot of room for me to continue to improve. So that's what excites me the most. I feel like I can continue to get a lot better. And before we know it, I'm sure we'll all be back here and ready for the next year."

And with that Clark got up out of her chair, already checking her phone before she'd left the podium. The Sun fell in the WNBA semifinals in five games. Even though the games were even more important, the Sun did not sell out either of their WNBA semifinals home games after packing Mohegan Sun Arena for both playoff games against the Fever.

For her work turning a five-win team the year before she arrived as head coach into a 13-win team in 2023 and a 20-win playoff team in 2024, Sides received a vote for 2024 Coach of the Year…and was fired a few weeks later. The Fever decided they needed a coach with playoff experience and to address the defense, and an Indiana legend, White, let it be known she'd be willing to leave Connecticut and come home. It certainly didn't hurt that Clark has tremendous admiration for White.

The woman who hired her was not Dunn, who had completed her three-year project, putting Indiana on a path to contending once again. At 77 she was ready to retire—or so she said. Instead, longtime Fever executive Kelly Krauskopf, who'd been hired away by the Indiana Pacers, returned to her women's basketball roots with a far bigger task ahead and a canvas to do it. Along with new GM Amber Cox, another longtime WNBA executive, the Fever aimed to maximize all the energy Clark had brought to the team, turning it into a winner on the court and igniting the fanbase.

During White's introductory press conference in November 2024, reporters asked her about how she planned to take the playoff-bound Fever and turn them into the championship Fever. "Offensively, we can be more creative," White said. "We can utilize more versatility, utilize certain players in different ways. I'm a forward-thinking, outside-the-box kind of coach…. They are a high-IQ team, so also giving them the freedom to make plays like we want to make plays, don't run plays."

If that sounds like the style of offense Bluder ran at Iowa, the style of offense the Van Horne Hornettes pioneered under Larry Wiebke, you're not mistaken. Clark was present for White's introduction. She was a regular presence in Indiana during the offseason, working in the gym at getting better, promoting her team and her many endorsement deals. She proved who she knew herself to be on the court, and the infrastructure that created the conditions for her success allowed her to take a settled place in the sports hierarchy with her financial future assured before she turned 23 years old.

CHAPTER FIVE

Caitlin Clark's Fairy Godmother

By the fall of 1972, Carroll Rugland had assumed an elder statesman level as the wildly successful head coach at Montezuma High School. He'd left Bennett Community School after the 1962–63 season, moving around 100 miles west and taking his new team to heights beyond even his Bennett state tournament runs. His Mounties won 89 straight games en route to 1969 and 1970 Iowa state titles before falling in the 1971 state final to Bud McLearn's Mediapolis squad 104–103.

So when he heard that Jim Schnack had taken the girls basketball job at Moravia High School, he summoned Schnack to his house, where the two men caught up over shared experiences, and Rugland gave Schnack a scouting report about his new job. Rugland had coached Jim's older sister, Bonny, back at Bennett, which was Schnack's alma mater. By virtue of his coaching clinics and work at summer camps all over the state, Rugland had an encyclopedic knowledge of not just which players were stars today but who was best positioned to rise to that level next.

Schnack had been informed by many, including the administrators who hired him, that he faced a rebuilding job at Moravia. The Mohawkettes had lost six seniors, including leading scorer Fonda Dicks. But when Schnack told this to Rugland, he dismissed this idea immediately.

"He said, 'You're going to have one of the best forwards in the state: Molly Van Benthuysen,'" Schnack recalled in a September 2024 phone interview. "'She's going to be really, really good.' Well, she only averaged, I think, 55 points per game for me."

Anyone who knew basketball understood that to see Van Benthuysen play once was to experience the kind of player who'd never been seen before. She had the kind of game, broad-based offensive skills, and relentless work ethic that allowed her to push the boundaries of what was possible on the court. I told Lisa Bluder that Van Benthuysen had been on hand to watch her Iowa team defeat South Carolina in the 2023 Final Four for Caitlin Clark's signature win. "Machine Gun Molly was here?" Bluder said giddily. "[I] didn't even know that. I watched her with the Iowa Cornets. Are you kidding?"

Even after a late night, Bluder treated me to a monologue on what Van Benthuysen and six-on-six meant. "Iowa basketball," Bluder said, "I know some people can't understand it, six-on-six. I played it. Coach Jensen played it. Coach Fitzgerald played it. It was so much fun. It was a scorer's game. Coach Jensen scored 105 points in one game.

Her average in high school was 66 points a game, just crazy stuff. But it was really fun, and you really learned how to shoot the ball. You learned how to be an offensive-minded person. Don't ask us about defense, but we could shoot the ball. So I think that sticks with you a little bit. We still love our offense. I know, I think we played some pretty good defense last night. Everybody keeps knocking our defense. I thought our defense was pretty good last night, but offense is near and dear to us old six-on-sixers' hearts."

Calling Van Benthuysen a "forward" incidentally doesn't mean the same thing in the six-on-six game as it does in today's five-player teams. Six-on-six meant designating three players, typically your three most defensive-oriented players, as guards, who stayed on the half of the court the opponent was shooting at, while three forwards played offense for your team.

But Van Benthuysen came of age at a moment everything was changing in women's basketball in ways that tested the progress of what so many pioneers had built, forced a rethinking of everything from what the game meant to girls, and ultimately altered the basic structure of gameplay in Iowa itself, though the residual effects of six-on-six continue to fuel the progress of women's basketball to this day. Molly Van Benthuysen, then Molly Bolin, now Molly Kazmer, who showed women's basketball so much of what was possible, though, had the grave misfortune of living just a few decades too soon to live it herself.

Molly was born Monna Van Benthuysen on November 13, 1957, in Dryden, Ontario, the fifth of six children to Forrest and Wanda Van Benthuysen. Forrest worked pipeline for a living, and that meant an itinerant life for his family, who moved first to Phoenix, where Molly lived until the end of her second-grade year. But both of her parents were Iowa natives, and when Molly's grandmother (her mother's mother) died, her family moved back to Iowa to take care of her grandfather first in New Sharon, then settling in Moravia, where Molly's dad got a job helping to construct Rathbun Dam.

Molly's entire life trajectory changed. "Oh, my gosh, that was just everything," she said in a June 2024 interview. "I mean, if I hadn't been back there, I probably would have ended up in a sport, but undoubtedly it wouldn't have been basketball. The options, when you have a large family and not a lot of money—they're not going to pay for stuff, so golf is out. Tennis is out. You've got to have memberships to do any of that stuff, and it had to be offered in school. So for [me] it was to learn a sport for free, or you weren't going to get to play."

Forrest's idea of sports was hunting and fishing. Molly's mom didn't play anything at all. But placed in Iowa, she did get to see her older sister, Dolly, play basketball. Molly learned to twirl a baton at an early age, a skill she has maintained to this day. "I've got a baton in my bedroom," she said, laughing. But more than anything, Molly wanted attention and fame as a young girl. And so the experience when she was in fifth grade, attending a Moravia High School girls basketball game in the girls basketball capital of the world, set her on her life's path.

Moravia's population checked in at 699 in the 1970 U.S. Census, and that's roughly where it was since 1900 (632) and also now (637 in 2020). And so Molly remembers a childhood of quiet, wandering in the fields looking at clouds, going to the pond, and trying to catch a bullfrog or spending hours reading headstones in the cemetery located across the street from her house.

But armed with her baton, she was part of the halftime entertainment for a Moravia High School girls basketball game, one in which one of her older sisters, Jonna (nicknamed Jolly) was a cheerleader, and another older sister, Donna (nicknamed Dolly) played on the team, and she found entry into an exciting world she'd never even imagined. "I just remember being in that gym," Molly recalled. "It was *packed*, and the pep band was playing, and there's popcorn smell in the air, and people were cheering and going crazy. And it was a close game, and the whole gym just reverberated, and I was like, *Wow—now this is an electric atmosphere.*"

There weren't youth teams for Molly to join back then, so she got her basketball fix in a few ways. She'd convince her older sisters—Dolly was five years older, Jolly was four years ahead of Molly—to let her tag along to watch the Moravia High School team play. She'd get the chance to play in games during physical education classes in school. And she shot for hours and hours by herself on a local hoop in town to prepare for the one game a year she knew she'd get to play in front of people—the Family Fun Night in Moravia, where the fifth graders faced off against the sixth graders. She led the game in scoring both years she was eligible to play, then quickly joined the junior high school team in seventh grade. She starred for the junior high team coached by her next-door neighbor, Richard Pauley, who let her shoot into the bent-rimmed hoop on his driveway, which Molly would do for hours every day, wanting nothing more than to play for Moravia High and lead her team to the state tournament. "The whole town talked about the girls team winning and everything," Molly said. "So I was hearing it all around me, and it was quite obvious that if you want to be successful or become somebody or take a step up in the world, that you needed to play basketball."

Molly was the kind of kid to find anything to compete in. She entered an anti-litter poster and essay contest in sixth grade just for the thrill of perhaps winning it. In seventh grade she played clarinet in a solo music contest. She gave an illustrated talk before 4H as an eighth grader on vegetable plates and salads. "Nobody notices you're even in the room," Molly said. "I had that especially when I was a teenager with some lower self-esteem, that I wanted to break out of and prove myself. So I was that kind of person."

All this time she never stopped working on her game. And she'd go to any lengths to get better. Take the girls basketball camp at Parsons College. The visionary girls and women's basketball coach, Bob Spencer, ran the camp. But the $75 cost of the camp was beyond the means of Molly's parents. Still only 13 years old, Van Benthuysen tried everything she could to earn enough money to attend the camp. She was too young to get her working papers, but she found a magazine that would let her sell Christmas and greeting cards door to door. Between that and taking out an ad in the *Moravia Union* offering her babysitting services, she racked up $25. It wasn't enough, she cried to her junior high coach, Richard Pauley.

So Pauley wrote a letter to Spencer, explaining the dilemma, and the answer came back from Spencer to Van Benthuysen directly. "It said, 'If you would like to come work in the lunch line or serving the food line, it won't take very much of your time, and you'll enjoy it. I'll just take the deposit. You can come to camp,'" she said. "I mean, I still have that letter today. It was the best day of my life."

Van Benthuysen worked and she played, sweeping the awards for Mikan Drill, the Lane Drill, and the Most Improved Set Shot. She estimated she spent nine hours a day in the gym each day of camp. Her only breaks came when she served in the food line for meals. "I went all out," Van Benthuysen said. "I wanted to win everything. I wanted to win every prize they had. And the director was watching me."

On the Thursday of her week in the camp, Spencer called her into his office. She entered, trembling. *What had she done wrong?* "I'm impressed with your work ethic and how hard you try and that you're always on time for your job," Spencer said. "Would you like to come back again next week and do the same?" Van Benthuysen didn't have to be asked twice. Spencer called her parents, and she stayed over the weekend with the counselors, and that became her summer home—first as essentially a Spencer scholarship figure, then as a paid counselor, earning $50 a week.

Spencer's camp had an ulterior motive. As the head coach at Parsons, he was using it as recruiting tool, the kind that is taken for granted today, but at the time just ahead of Title IX, it was a rare thing for anyone to experience. For Van Benthuysen it was a car ride away. And several head coaches of Iowa high school teams saw her at camp and knew what kind of player she was, including, of course, Rugland.

Meanwhile, high school offered Van Benthuysen a full range of experiences, and she answered yes to every one of them: science club, pep club, Future Homemakers of America, other sports, too—she excelled at the high jump—with basketball, of course, first on her list. Van Benthuysen was living out the ideal of the Iowa girls basketball model presented to the world.

But even as Van Benthuysen chased glory to great acclaim, another Iowa girls basketball player fought for her seat at the table.

In the spring of 1970, Ruthven High School sophomore Jane Christoffer finished her season with a scoring average of nearly 47 points per game. She also found out she was pregnant by her longtime boyfriend, classmate Ken Rubel. The two married in July of 1970, and Jennifer, their daughter, was born on December 5. The following month, she met with Ruthven officials to discuss returning to the team. But they couldn't let her. The Iowa Girls High School Athletic Union (IGHSAU) had a rule forbidding married women or mothers from playing high school girls basketball, and Jane was both.

Since there was no rule against married men or fathers playing, Jane filed suit against the IGHSUA and E. Wayne

Cooley, alleging a violation of her civil rights. She had the support of her town as well—reports at the time included statements of support from the school administrators, local townspeople, even Emma Ruthven—granddaughter of the man who founded the town of Ruthven—herself. By November of 1971, a judge ruled she could practice with her team while the suit proceeded, and a few weeks later, with visions of legal fees destroying the IGHSUA's budget, Cooley reversed the rule, though he made it clear in his public comments he didn't agree with the decision or the rationale behind it. "I remember being programmed to the point where you wouldn't dream of ever stepping out of line and losing your chance to play if you love the game," Van Benthuysen recalled from that time. "So it was a way of controlling the behavior of girls in high school, which sports is a great way to keep you on track with school and your education and not getting into a lot of trouble.... There was just this hidden thing of control that I don't think a lot of us realized at the time that was going on behind the scenes."

It is something she realized later on, when her own life created a scenario that put even more of what she cared about into question. At the time, though? "I don't remember a lot about that when I was a teenager except for the fact that because we were so programmed that I thought, *Oh, she stepped out of line. Too bad.* I didn't even have that awareness or that other side because in my world I felt like I was being treated fairly because I followed the rules. And I felt you can't do that or you're out," Van Benthuysen said. "So it wasn't until I was much older and had more of a sense of self in my own beliefs, separate from what I was being programmed to be, that I saw that and experienced it myself, the unfairness of it, and I didn't realize all this time while acting publicly—'Look what we do for these girls. Look what they get to do. They get to go to the state tournament, they get to play, they get their uniforms, they get to travel, they get buses, they get all this stuff. And look what we do for them.' But then the underside of that is you step out of the line, you're out if you don't do what we say. So it was a little jarring when that reality set in."

Still, Van Benthuysen sees the benefit of Iowa girls basketball—rules and all—to this day. "Still, if the IGHSAU hadn't formed in 1925, Iowa, like the rest of the country, would have the girls teams playing school sports noncompetitively like a PE class," she said. "We were fortunate to get to compete in those days and received equality with the boys for gym time and for uniforms and equipment *long* before anyone else in the country did! Thousands of Iowa high school girls over the years enjoyed playing basketball in gyms packed full of fans."

It took time for Van Benthuysen to get her chance in high school basketball. Her Moravia team had that group of six—the ones whose losses Schnack had been told would be catastrophic to his chances as head coach—and Van Benthuysen stood just 5'4" as a freshman. Relegated to the junior varsity team, she averaged 33 points per game there while waiting for her chance to shine. When she was a sophomore, the group of six seniors largely froze her out, she remembered, putting her in the back behind all the taller seniors so she couldn't be seen in a photo they took, even though she'd been feeding them the ball all night. Still, serving as the third forward, she averaged 25 points per game, and Moravia fell just three points shy of reaching the state tournament.

Despite the size of the town, Moravia never lacked for players to join the high school varsity basketball team. "Moravia, I think I had 30 girls," Schnack recalled. He wasn't surprised. It was baked into the culture, particularly in small towns. Schnack's mother, then Gerry Dittmer, had played for Durant back in the 1930s.

But Van Benthuysen immediately asserted herself as one of the very best in the state her junior season, scoring 63 points in her first game. It didn't hurt that she'd sprouted up to 5'8" by then. Listed at 5'10", she had a wingspan and form that made her shot impossible to block.

By December 20, 1973, her local paper needed to explain away a poor performance of hers: "The Moravia girls scored another win at Seymour Friday night 71–56, but the boys weren't able to score from the free-throw line and lost 62–49. In the girls games, Molly Van Benthuysen, who is one of the state's highest scorers, was nursing a sprained ankle and wound up with only 42 points, while she has been averaging 53.6 points a game so far this season."

Ah yes, only 42 points. What a disappointment. But this is how Van Benthuysen came to be understood as a phenomenon. The goal, without fail, was simple: get to the state tournament and win it. "The Iowa girls basketball high school state tournament was the epitome of success for me," Van Benthuysen said, "because you went to Des Moines, you rode the bus, you got out of school for a week, you stay in a hotel. Your photos were displayed in the glass case of a downtown store where they could see your team, and you were queens for a week. I mean, that was the ultimate goal for me when I was in high school."

But then what? "Nothing beyond," she said. "There was no Olympic team, right? There were very limited college teams with scholarships, almost none. So for me to even think about going on a scholarship wasn't even on my radar, and then I knew I couldn't afford college. So I would have to work, and I may not be able to afford college. So the focus for me was getting into that state tournament. That's what I lived for."

Depending on which newspaper you preferred, Van Benthuysen finished either on the all-state second or fourth team. After falling to Wayne in the district semifinals—Van Benthuysen scored 64, but Rhonda Cobb hit a last-second shot to beat Moravia 85–84—Van Benthuysen and Moravia had one more shot at Iowa glory. And by then the attention had swelled considerably. Reporters swarmed her games. A documentary filmmaker followed her and her Moravia team around. Van Benthuysen starred for the softball team in the fall, made honor roll, and then moved swiftly toward what she believed was destiny.

She did it without Schnack, who received what he described as "a blank check offer" to coach and teach at Keokuk High School and start the girls basketball program. He still regrets accepting that job. "Hindsight is always 20/20," Schnack said. "I probably should have stayed at Moravia one more year at least. Molly was coming back. She would have been a senior."

But the game in Iowa was changing rapidly, and there were no real ways to know what was about to happen to the landscape. Keokuk, population 14,631 in the 1970 census, needed to start a girls basketball team because the law of the land in the United States as of June 23, 1972, was Title IX.

Although hundreds of small schools across Iowa had long supported girls basketball, suddenly the decision to do so was no longer optional. The 1973 girls basketball season featured for the first time schools from Des Moines. Washington High School in Cedar Rapids even reached the state tournament. And when the larger school districts looked for coaches to hire, naturally, they went after the most innovative and successful small school minds to do it. As Rugland saw it, the larger schools were "a force to be reckoned with."

Part of the dizzying array of changes Van Benthuysen experienced throughout her playing career at every level, Ivan Hankins took over in Moravia for her senior year. Such turnover was a consequence of the times she lived in just as surely as it was for Dorcas Andersen or Clark.

The level of Molly's scoring still kept rising. By January 24, 1975, she'd registered 83 points in a win aginst Central Decatur of Leon. That was one of the highest single-game marks since Denise Long scored 111 in a game back in 1968, though Long, who went on to be drafted by the NBA's Golden State Warriors, lived as the classic center in Iowa six-on-six lore, while Van Benthuysen scored from, well, everywhere. By then, Van Benthuysen had hit another two game-winners for Moravia, and Hankins described her as "an absolute pleasure to coach…. She has to be one of the best who has ever played the game."

She scored 70 in her last home game against Mormon Trail, too. But it wasn't quite enough, and Moravia lost 95–94. Instead of capturing that moment of triumph, the camera crew in the locker room showed viewers an absolutely distraught Van Benthuysen sobbing on the locker room floor before being helped up off the ground by her best friend, teammate Lisa Clark (now Fetters). Van Benthuysen always kept her composure, especially in public. But the moment was too big for that. There'd be no state tournament for Van Benthuysen. She thought her basketball career was over.

But the very changes that roiled Iowa girls basketball, and really the entire women's sports landscape, were present at the state tournament in her senior season as well. What began as an informal recruiting process each year, as colleges began to add women's basketball, was formalized by Cooley with the addition of a room for the 24 colleges, including two from out of state, who attended the state tournament and set up shop in a second-floor room at Vets Auditorium. "This hospitality room for prospective students and athletes has gone over so big that we may have to request double space next year," the man in charge of setting up the space, Rod Lein, told *The Des Moines Register* in March 1975. Not coincidentally, Lein was also the head coach at Grand View College. And he was positively beaming as he told the newspaper about two of his recruits, including Van Benthuysen. "I've already had a great week," Lein said.

Of course, those 24 schools all played five-on-five. Title IX contained the seeds of six-on-six's destruction. It is generally understood that there was nothing less about six-on-six, even though the rules were created for the purpose of limiting how hard girls, playing the game of basketball, had to work. The evolution of the game pushed by elite athleticism turned it into what is effectively a pair of high-speed, three-on-three matchups. The enduring entertainment of three-on-three has surprised many people and continues to this day, even emerging as an Olympic sport.

But those origins, combined with the national landscape post-Title IX—at every other level, five-on-five was the dominant set of basketball rules—meant that both practically and philosophically, Iowa was out of step with the very opportunities to play basketball sprouting up overnight across the world in both the collegiate and professional ranks. It is something the first head coach of University of Iowa for women's basketball, Lark Birdsong, saw right away. "There were some conversations I had with other people about Iowa," Birdsong said in September 2024. "I was a proponent for Iowa moving to the five-player game because I could just see down the horizon. If they didn't, none of their girls were going to be considered for scholarships, and it was so embedded and so successful that I was also told that they would never switch because why, in essence, why mess with success? But there was a greater course going on, and eventually they did change."

That took a good 20 years, legal action, and ultimately a decision by Cooley in the early 1990s. Popular sentiment by then had just crossed over into favoring the decision, but many of those lament the decision to this day. Notably, though, the game itself has directly influenced the way Iowa plays five-on-five in ways that are clear in Clark's game, too.

That was true for Van Benthuysen with the not-insignificant difference that she had to come directly from the six-on-six game and effectively learn the new rules on the fly as she played the five-on-five game her freshman season at Grand View under Lein. By AIAW (Association for Intercollegiate Athletics for Women) tournament time, she was Grand View's No. 1 scorer.

Her patron for summer camps, Spencer, coached at William Penn University in Oskaloosa, Iowa. He unsuccessfully encouraged Van Benthuysen to finish her two years at Grand View so that she could transfer to William Penn. The players, who'd led William Penn to the AIAW national semifinals before falling to the dynasty that was Cathy Rush's Immaculata, would graduate by then. "And then we played

William Penn and beat them," Van Benthuysen recalled with a laugh.

That 61–46 win was televised on the Iowa Educational Broadcast Network. The following night, Grand View played Birdsong's Iowa Hawkeyes and beat them 112–53. This is only confusing in hindsight. At the time Grand View was the better basketball program. Iowa had hired the legendary Christine Grant as "associate professor and athletic director—women" in 1973. Grant's tireless efforts on behalf of women's sports helped make Iowa a haven for women athletes but in a way that never prioritized basketball, or any other sport, above the rest. So while Grant fought for and often won additional funding for women's sports, she then distributed it equally. Birdsong was not provided recruiting funding of any kind since no other women's sport at Iowa was. In fact, when Birdsong began it was against the rules of the AIAW, a national organization, which sprang up to support women's college athletics due to something between disinterest and active distaste from the NCAA at the time, to provide a college basketball program with such funds. Birdsong was given one scholarship—same as the other 11 sports—which she was told to split four ways. It was entirely understandable, even admirable. But it handicapped Iowa women's basketball at a time other schools had built-in advantages even in state. Northern Iowa's teacher program attracted many players, for instance, while Iowa State had better athletics facilities at the time.

The *Iowa City Press-Citizen* revealed Birdsong's views in December 1975: "She adds that she believes perhaps the small colleges, at this point in the history of women's sports, have an advantage over the larger schools in that the campus and the community are small enough that the woman athlete gets a lot of esteem, which she probably wouldn't right now at Iowa, for instance. Lark also thinks that many small colleges tend to be more advanced toward the funding of women's programs."

Birdsong ultimately took Grand View off the schedule entirely for the following year. She determined Iowa was not yet ready to compete with them. The Hawkeyes were not ready for Van Benthuysen, but they wouldn't have faced her the following season anyway. She'd married her high school sweetheart, Dennie Bolin, and gave birth to her son, Damien, in January 1977 before returning to Grand View. Still, her path was always rocky, often in ways entirely out of her control. Lein did not last the season at Grand View. He'd been hired to coach at Simpson College the following year and began recruiting players for his new team before his old team's season was complete. When administration caught wind of it, it let him go early. (Simpson beat Iowa in 1976–77, as did William Penn.)

Four weeks after she gave birth to Damien, Molly was still actively wondering if she wanted to keep playing basketball. Her financial aid, mostly grants and loans, were not dependent on playing basketball. She and Dennie had a small place in Colfax, just outside of Des Moines. "Somebody came and knocked at my door, and there was a church league, and they were missing a player, and they wanted to know if I'd fill in for the basketball game," Molly recalled. "I was like, 'Shoot, here I go. Here's a bottle.' I'm out the door. So I go in there and I score like 67 points in this church, destroyed these poor church ladies."

That was a moment—and Molly faced many of them—when she knew she would not give up basketball without a fight. "I just remember that first time back on the court, that feeling of like, this is where I belong," she said. "I love this. It's a big part of my life. I am not walking away."

So it was back to Grand View's team in 1977–78, though many of her teammates had dispersed by then. Dennie struggled to find work and was frequently at home with Damien. Molly juggled her responsibilities at home while taking a full course load and playing basketball. In a February 14, 1978, article in *The Des Moines Register* about the three of them, Dennie asserted that "Girls are too slow to play the five-on-five game" 12 days after Molly scored 42 in a five-on-five win against Iowa State.

But as her season ended, figuring out where to go next was anything but obvious. She'd studied communications at Grand View, felt natural and comfortable in front of the camera, but not a lot of people around the country knew who she was. For instance, she'd been invited to try out but hadn't made the 1976 USA Basketball women's Olympic team. And the women's college basketball landscape at this time—six years after Title IX was signed into law—was like a loose collection of bright lights shining in places around the country but without anything like a network connecting everyone. "I had two years of college eligibility left, and I was going, 'Damn, I don't want to live in cold weather. I'm gonna see if I can get into Arizona State or something' because I had some family and I had lived in Arizona," she said. "So I started communicating with the coaches there, and they were like, 'Well, who the hell are you? I've never heard of you, right? So if you want to walk on, you're welcome to walk on.' So that was my choice of being a walk-on. Go to Arizona and be a walk-on."

But another choice presented itself soon after. Her Grand View coach, Lein, had been hired as the general manager of the Iowa Cornets, a franchise in the Women's Professional Basketball League known as the WBL. And the first player he signed was Molly Bolin. "He knew my value after recruiting me from high school," she said. "And he knew I would bring value from a marketing standpoint, that I could handle interviews, that I could meet the press, that I would do the appearances. And he was a promoter to the max. So he called and said, 'Hey, we're starting a pro league. And we're gonna make a movie. You want to do it?' I'm like, 'Yeah, Sign me up!'"

If the business plan sounds scattered, well, it was. The Cornets signed Bolin, along with three other Iowa natives in Rhonda Penquite, Connie Kunzmann, and Mary Schrad, and in lieu of a single home court, they barnstormed around the state for its 17 home games. The movie—first called *Dribble*, then ultimately released as *Scoring*—featured few name actors, but Pete Maravich played himself, and the idea of women playing basketball was utilized for laughs or as simply a device to attract men in much of the film itself.

The team was owned by George Nissen, Cedar Rapids' own and an accomplished gymnast (he won three national championships at University of Iowa), who went on to have an epiphany for a new device, which he called a "trampoline." He made so much money with his 44 patents that he believed he could easily afford to pay the $50,000 franchise fee to join the WBL in 1978 and finance the team's $250,000 operating budget and finance the film, too.

By the month of June, Bolin, Nissen, and Lein found themselves in the Iowa governor's office holding a press conference while Bolin presented governor Robert Ray with a Cornets jersey, then signed the first WBL contract. Even on that day, she didn't hesitate to reflect on what her alternatives were had the WBL not come along. "If this hadn't come along, all I could have done was coach," she said on June 30, 1978. "I'd like to coach some day, but that day will come when I can't run up and down the floor. I just want to keep playing ball. When I graduated, I couldn't stand the thought of not playing. This came at a perfect time for me because I was free to do it. It's a perfect chance."

The basketball, ultimately, was at the highest level. League founder Bill Byrne imagined the league, which started in 1978, getting the extra attention from the 1980 Olympics to boost the league's finances. But the United States ultimately boycotted the 1980 Olympics, which had the silver lining of freeing up players like Ann Meyers and Carol Blazejowski to participate. Bolin more than held her own against these bigger names, winning co-MVP with Meyers in 1980, the league's second season. But she had to prove herself even in a circuit, which had made her the top pick.

The league utilized her to promote every chance it got, having her pose not only in her uniform but in a tank top and shorts. The result was some negativity from some in the larger public who saw the ads as sexist, though her teammates and opponents were mostly supportive. For Bolin there just was not enough money in a league trying to survive with low player salaries. So she forged her own way by being the first player to capitalize on sports marketing for extra income. "Women across the country were fighting for equality, we're only a few years into Title IX, and they are very offended that now all of a sudden the new women's pro basketball league is promoting sexism," said Long Beach State basketball player John Kazmer. "But the truth was sexism permeated society. That's why *Charlie's Angels* was such a hit show in the '70s! And the league didn't create it. The league was just trying to follow along what it seemed like society was looking for be successful."

Bolin even remembered having to prove herself on the court as well. Assistant coach Bruce Mason was a persistent voice, arguing to limit her playing time early in her first season because the six-on-six game she'd mastered in high school had kept her from learning how to play defense well enough to stay on the court. With only two non-consecutive years of college experience, she was still learning the full-court game when the Cornets began. She'd get a few minutes apiece in the first few games, not enough to find her shooting rhythm. Then about six games into the season, a teammate's injury allowed her more playing time, and she came off the bench and scored 38 in one half. That shut Mason up for good.

But Nissen turned out to be less solvent than he thought. He lost more than $1 million on the film, which quickly disappeared from theaters, and faced lawsuits over the safety of his trampolines. He had to sell his majority stake in the team and announced it the same day in the spring of 1979 that Bolin scored 53 points, the league single-game record, in Vets Auditorium in Des Moines. She finally had her state tournament moment.

When the game was over, her mother Wanda was so excited about her performance that she fainted. Dennie groused to a reporter postgame about how he'd wanted to go shopping that day, but Molly didn't want to—it was a gameday, after all. The two of them were drifting apart, Molly said, and Dennie's drinking became more frequent, his ability to find work became increasingly rare, and Molly's meager salaries playing basketball (plus $3 a pop from the autographed posters she sold) had to pay their bills.

By the start of the WBL's third season, there were too many signs that the league didn't have the financial wherewithal to survive. The Cornets offered Molly the same $14,000 she'd earned the year before despite winning co-MVP of the league honors with Meyers. Unfortunately, the Iowa Cornets, despite playing in two championships and having strong attendance records, were not able to secure new ownership and ceased operations by September 1980.

Molly decided to accept the $30,000 offer from Tony Mercurio, owner of the California Breeze, who were part of a new startup league—the LPBA. In late September of 1980, she moved out west with Dennie and Damien and immediately started promoting the team. She was invited to speak at a Los Angeles Lakers press conference and was introduced to Jerry Buss and Magic Johnson and attended Lakers games during the Showtime years as a VIP. Even with many WBL players joining the LPBA, Molly averaged 40 points a game in the few games the Breeze played until the entire league collapsed at the end of 1980. Dennie did not adjust to living in California. "He didn't try to put any effort into trying," Molly said. "We had a nice house, we had a condo we were staying in, but he didn't try to meet anybody, to try to find a job. He was not happy there and he blamed me for everything that his life was falling apart because he didn't know anyone. And he was a fish out of water out there."

By 1981 their marriage was over and so was the LPBA. In January of 1981, Molly fielded multiple offers from nearly every WBL team and returned to finish out the final season of the WBL out west on the San Francisco Pioneers. An Albuquerque crowd of 3,378 packed the arena to see Molly score a game-high 29 points in the All-Star Game. Even though she'd played only once before in Albuquerque, "We

Love You, Molly" signs were clearly visible during the game. "I loved it," Molly said following the game. "I've been here before and I guess I had a following."

By the playoffs, games against Nancy Lieberman's Dallas Diamonds drew north of 8,000 per game. The audience was there and growing. It just needed investment and time. None of it was enough, though. The WBL folded in the summer of 1981.

Molly believed her future was out west, but Dennie wanted no part of living there. A custody battle ensued. And everything Molly had done to try and build a professional basketball life was used against her in court. Her travel schedule playing basketball was entered into evidence. Her alluring posters were entered into evidence. And the small county court ultimately ruled in Dennie's favor, citing her demanding basketball career as the key issue in that decision.

The whispers grew in Moravia, too. Ostracized by their local community, Molly's parents had to stop attending their local church. And Molly picked up a $5-an-hour construction job with flexible hours and learned to paint, allowing her to take some more lucrative subcontracting gigs and build a life in California around making time for her son. But she only managed to appeal the loss of custody by getting an attorney to take the case for $500, and her parents had to drive with her to the attorney's office to deliver that money. The Iowa Supreme Court reversed the lower court's decision on July 20, 1983.

A few months before that, she'd toured the country with a group of elite women's basketball players in Nancy Lieberman's Ladies Over America All Star Basketball Tour. Here's how her biography in that program read in February 1983:

MOLLY BOLIN—San Francisco Pioneers.

Three-year pro. A high school All-American, Molly averaged 54.8 PPG and hit a record high of 83 points as a senior. She attended Grand View College in Des Moines before signing pro with the Iowa Cornets. She played in two championship finals and was a three-time All-Pro and All-Star selection. Molly was 1980 co-MVP (with Ann Meyers) of WBL and scoring champ with 32.8 PPG. She set WBL Scoring record three times with games of 53, 54, and 55. The all-time leading scorer in women's basketball is now working construction in Riverside.

Let that last line sink in. That's what it meant to be Caitlin Clark in 1983.

In the summer of 1984, Molly was recruited to play with the USA All-Star team formed to tour and help prepare the women's Olympic Basketball team coached by Pat Summitt that was on its way to gold at the 1984 games in

Los Angeles. The All-Star team consisted of the top players who had played professionally and were no longer eligible for the Olympic team. This included many players who were on the 1980 Olympic team that missed out on the competition due to the USA boycott, such as the first Wade Trophy winners Lieberman and Carol Blazejowski. A July 10 double-header featuring men's and women's versions of All-Stars vs. Olympians (which the women Olympians won easily, 97–54) drew 67,596 people, at that point the largest crowd to ever watch an indoor basketball game...at the Hoosier Dome in Indianapolis, two miles from where Clark would draw sellout crowds throughout the 2024 WNBA season 40 years later. "They had this huge, big screen, and Ronald Reagan welcomed everybody on the screen, and then they had the Olympic flags and the themes and all that," Molly said. "That whole experience of training at the Olympic training center for a week with the All-Star team and then going on tour was the only Olympics I was ever going to get."

Within a three-month span in 1984, Molly played in front of more than 67,000 people at the Hoosier Dome; got selected by the New York team in the WABA; shot a commercial with Larry Bird; was told the New York team had already folded; got sent to Columbus, Ohio, in the dispersal draft; and picked up and headed back east to resume her career in the WABA in Ohio. Her mother, Wanda, travelled out west and cared for Damien as she gave it another shot. "It is sometimes frustrating," she told *The Des Moines Register*'s Chuck Offenburger in October 1984, to "still be fighting the same battles getting the women's pro game started up as we were fighting when we tried it six years ago, but I really believe it's eventually going to catch on."

The WABA lasted only one year, better than the NWBA, which started up in 1986. Molly had been burned too many times and wanted some say in operations. So they made her assistant commissioner. She invited Iowa governor Terry Branstad to a press conference and, of course, he attended. That's the power of Machine Gun Molly. When she got back home to California from the press conference, the check from the NWBA arrived to reimburse her for the trip—and it bounced. Molly was told that Lieberman, also involved in the league, had run up too high of a room service bill. The NWBA never played a game. "What's so bad is that you keep thinking there's going to be a tomorrow," Molly said in September 2024. "And you're trying to stay in shape and stay active and play competitively, mostly men's leagues."

It never happened for Molly. She never stopped innovating, holding coaching clinics for decades, coming up with new business ideas. She proposed a made-for-TV, three-on-three basketball tournament starring the best women's players and even found a national television outlet for it in

Liberty Sports. If that sounds identical to the business plan for Unrivaled, just 30 years ahead of its time, that's because it is. But that was cut short because Liberty got scared off by the big new league that had just been proposed: the WNBA. "I got a phone call," she said. "Basically, 'Hey, we're not going to compete with that.'"

It was hard for Molly to make peace with the WNBA's rise early in the league's tenure. She'd written to the league, hoping to get involved, but never heard back. Even when a former WBLer, Donna Orender, took the reins as WNBA president, the league didn't find a home for her professionally. "It's hard to explain to somebody that has opportunities what it's like to have experienced it and have it yanked away that fast," she said, "because we believed in it."

She, though, had found love long before. She met her husband, Kazmer, at a softball game in 1988. Kazmer fielded a ball in the outfield and—after seeing Molly was the one covering second base—lollipop'd the throw back to the infield. Molly took exception, and as he trotted back to his position in the outfield, she pegged the ball right between his shoulder blades.

"I said, 'Next time, throw the damn ball,'" Molly said, laughing. "He said he lobbed it on purpose and then threw it as hard as he could, and it was right along the ground like that, and I snapped it off. I said, 'Now *that's* a throw.' He's like, 'I've got to meet this person.' So that's how we got started."

They've been together ever since and celebrated their 35th wedding anniversary in November 2024. Molly Kazmer started to make her peace with the WNBA when she was invited by Orender to the 2006 WNBA All-Star Game in Madison Square Garden. She'd played in the 1979 WBL version of the game, the first-ever pro All-Star Game, though it was hastily arranged just a few weeks ahead of time. It was shown on WOR-TV, and the crowd on hand was 2,731. In comparison 13,000 people showed up for the 2006 event, which was nationally televised on ESPN.

Kazmer serves on the board now of Legends of the Ball, a group founded by Liz Galloway-McQuitter, the Alana Beard of the WBL—she led the circuit in steals and was roundly considered the best perimeter defender the league ever saw—to raise awareness of what the WBL did to pave the way for the WNBA and women's basketball. And, of course, there simply wouldn't have been a WBL without Kazmer. There are still many who don't know it, but she and her fellow LOB officers were introduced on the big screen at the 2024 WNBA All-Star Game. That crowd in Phoenix dwarfed even the 2006 event in New York, and she took in the celebration of Clark and the rest of today's stars, even stopping to take a photo with Clark's parents,

Brent and Anne, just Iowa royalty greeting one another amid the festivities. "I'm like her fairy godmother that she never knew existed," Molly said, laughing, "because someone had to come wave that magic wand for about 20, 30 years and be the first to break down social barriers and continue the fight to get to where we are today with women's pro basketball."

Meanwhile, back in Moravia, the town understands just what she meant to Iowa, to girls and women's basketball, to Moravia itself. She was inducted into the Moravia Wall of Fame in 2013 and spoke to a packed Moravia High gymnasium. And you cannot drive through Moravia, population 626 as of 2023, without seeing Molly Kazmer on the town mural right next to the post office on the downtown square. Her long arms extend in that impossible-to-block motion as her teammates and a football player, too, watch her take another shot. We dreamed the same dreams," Kazmer said. "We fought the same battles except the opportunities weren't just quite ready there yet, and we didn't know that at the time. We didn't know what it was going to take. God, I don't know, if someone had pulled me aside as a 20 year old and said, 'Oh, by the way, you're going to be 60 before anybody's going to pay any attention to women for basketball,' I would have said, 'I don't believe it, I don't believe it. I can make it happen.' But who knew?"

CHAPTER SIX

Who Gets a Rope Line?

The most celebrated and watched women's college basketball player made her debut and not a single paying customer witnessed it. No, this is not because the University of Iowa lacked a passionate fanbase for women's basketball. Quite the contrary: in 2019–20 the Hawkeyes ranked 10th in the country in average home attendance, with 7,102 fans per game showing up to Carver-Hawkeye Arena. That in itself was nothing new, as Iowa routinely found itself with a pair of schools, Iowa and Iowa State, in the top 10 for attendance.

But COVID-19 did strange things to historic events, and the ban on fans meant that a few staffers, some brave journalists, and the two benches witnessed Kate Martin pitch the ball to Caitlin Clark at the top of the key, Clark immediately penetrating into the lane and drawing the foul, her body making a loud thud against the floor before Martin and Monika Czinano lifted her up to take her free throws.

When it was over, Iowa had beaten Northern Iowa 96–81 to avenge a loss the season before. Clark's plays were punctuated by longtime Carver-Hawkeye public-address announcer Dave Gallagher's exhortations, which were particularly strange, echoing in an empty arena. When the game ended, all the Hawkeyes waved to the "audience" as Gallagher shouted, "Thanks Hawks! Thanks Hawks! Thanks Hawks!" Clark allowed herself a small smile at the dress rehearsal for what was to come.

It was a vintage Clark performance from the get-go. She entered college with room to grow, but she was already a player built for exceptions. Clark became only the second freshman to start every game in Lisa Bluder's first 21 seasons at the helm at Iowa. "You'd better be ready to guard her when she crosses the half-court line," Bluder said back in October before Clark's freshman season began. "She's a player that loves to shoot the ball and has tremendous range. I think sometimes her passing gets overlooked. We have had so many oh, wow moments in practice already, highlight-type passes. We had one today. Put that in the highlight film already because it was so unbelievable. I think sometimes people overlook how good of a passer she is just because she's such a tremendous scorer."

She scored 27 points, going 10-for-17 from the field and three-of-six from three-point range, and grabbed eight rebounds, dished out four assists, and even collected three steals. Neither Bluder nor Clark seemed to think it was particularly remarkable after it was over, though the line of questioning reflected how flabbergasted the reporters, many of whom got their first look at Clark that night, were. "She was what we expected," Bluder said. "She's so good with the ball in her hands. We've recruited her for so long, and we've been looking forward to this day for so long."

Added Clark: "I set my goals pretty high. I wouldn't say I'm shocked. It was a good start for sure."

She'd visualized what she wanted to happen on the court and then proceeded to make it so. It was no different a week later, when she scored 30 and dished out 13 assists in a 103–97 win against Drake a day after Bluder warned her that she "was going to have a target on her back now." It didn't matter; Bluder and Jan Jensen's alma maters had been vanquished.

In her third game, Clark scored 23 against Wisconsin and considered it an off night.

I caught up with Bluder after Clark's first three games and reminded her of what she'd told me before the season. "Well, I may not be the one that looks for her to score, but *she* has different ideas sometimes," Bluder said with a chuckle. "And she will look to score. And I wouldn't expect anything differently from Caitlin. That's the type of player she is. I mean, she's explosive offensively. I want her to look for her shot. But I also just need her to understand a good shot from a great shot, and there is a difference, especially at this level. And when the people that you're surrounded by, and that's different, and like you say, 'It's only three games into the year, and what she's been doing is remarkable.' And I'm so happy for her. But it's going to be a work in progress."

Looking back on those early days, Bluder believes a younger version of herself might not have been able to maximize Clark. "I had to have a lot of confidence to coach Caitlin," she said in a July 2024 interview. "You have to. And I think she would have run over a young and inexperienced coach. I think she would have run over them. And I think, too, there are some coaches she couldn't have played for because…there is some give and take. I think there's give and take with star players. And you've got to figure out as a coach what line you're going to walk. And I think I said, 'You can't say whoa to a racehorse.' To me I can't hold her back. And I kept telling that to my staff: 'Let's not put the bushel over the light. Okay, let's make sure we let that light shine and make sure, yes, we're going to hold her accountable, but we also don't want to dampen her spirit because that's what makes her great is that competitiveness, that fire, that passion. Let's not take that away from her, that freedom, let's not take that away from her, but yes, we're going to hold her accountable in these areas.'"

Lisa's husband, David, could tell right away that the partnership was working, too. "She would do a lot of things beautifully, and then she'd make some mistakes and do some things. And first year she'd come in and sit with Lisa after the game and said, 'Teach me,'" David recalled in an August 2024 interview. "And they'd sit down, and that's the incredible thing. Caitlin, she's really bright, really smart, and then she also wants to learn. I mean, a lot of these players think they know everything…. But she would come in, and they would just go through, watch game film, and see what she should do in this certain circumstance. And she would just, she'd just learn. And it took her a while. 'I know what I should do, but I didn't do it anyway.' And so she got to the point where she knew and did what she was supposed to do. And that was a cool thing to watch actually because freshman Caitlin was sloppy, beautiful at times, and artistic and amazing but sloppy, and that changed, and it changed everything."

Much of the work, it should be noted, came not on basketball technique but how to harness the frustration she'd feel from an official's call or a teammate's mistake.

Arguably the first signature Clark performance came in the Cy-Hawk Classic in Iowa City against Iowa State. At Carver-Hawkeye Arena, Iowa trailed by 17 points before Clark led a fourth-quarter comeback. The Cyclones still led 80–79 when Clark took the ball at the top of the key. Madison Wise, who had two inches on her, guarded Clark. Wise moved over the screen from Czinano and had a hand in Clark's face as she shot, fading away from 27 feet out. Didn't matter. Swish. Hawkeyes win. "Caitlin Clark put their team on her back and made some great plays," Iowa State head coach Bill Fennelly, a disciple of Bob Spencer, said after the game.

And Bluder identified the Molly Bolin-like belief in herself in Clark. "You want that confident swagger in a young player," Bluder said postgame. "You want that belief at a high level, and she has it. To have it as a freshman, such a young player, that's a great thing."

Again, the remarkable thing was how quickly the impossible became the expected. "Everybody is going to have off nights," Clark said after posting a triple-double, Iowa's first since Sam Logic in 2015, in a 92–65 win against Western Illinois. But it was also one of only three games all season in which she scored fewer than 20 points. She dished out at least four assists in all but one of her freshman-year contests. She had seven or more rebounds in 14 different games even as a lead guard.

By early January Coach Bluder was comparing her to Logic, an eventual first-round WNBA pick, and current WNBA big Megan Gustafson, who make up the historic royalty of the Iowa program. "Sam was just a different type of point guard," Bluder said in January 2021. "They're two completely different types of point guards. So, it's really hard to judge them or compare them because they were, they're so different…. But she's certainly one of the best freshmen that we've had. Certainly one of the best freshmen that's ever, you know, come in and contributed immediately. Even Megan Gustafson, who left as the National Player of the Year, didn't start until really around Christmas time or even a couple of games into the Big Ten season. So she's in some pretty good company."

Clark scored 37 on January 6, 2021, while Martin played with a broken nose in a win against Minnesota. Clark began a run of five straight 30-point games on February 4, finishing it on February 23 in a 111–93 loss to Maryland. The offense was still well ahead of defense for these Hawkeyes, who would finish 338th of 349 Division I teams in defensive efficiency in Clark's freshman year. (In the Maryland game, a young freshman big for the Terrapins named Angel Reese came off the bench, but absolutely nobody noted this matchup between Clark and Reese at the time.)

Ultimately, that defense would put a ceiling on Clark's freshman season. Iowa made a deep run in the Big Ten Tournament but allowed 104 to Diamond Miller's Terrapins in the final to fall short of a conference tournament crown. And Iowa reached the Sweet 16 in the NCAA Tournament but lost to Paige Bueckers and UConn 92–72. Clark recorded 21 points and five assists, but all five UConn starters would eventually play in the pros, and the Hawkeyes didn't really have an answer for any of them. "There was a true belief we were going to make the Final Four someday," said Clark, bringing up her goal from Signing Day. "We didn't say we were going to do it in my first year. We knew it was going to be a process. We had to put all the pieces together. To see what we did this year with nobody believing in us, we believed in ourselves. Everybody in the locker room, the coaches, the girls, we just kept believing. We had some tough losses but went back to work every single day and wanted to get better. I think that really showed at the end of the season through the Big Ten Tournament, obviously the NCAA Tournament. To get to where we got is really something special. Obviously, a lot to be proud of this season."

And something else happened, too: the game got flexed by ESPN onto ABC. "Somebody told me this was the first network televised game since 1995 when we played actually in the championship game against Tennessee," UConn coach Geno Auriemma said, making a point in his patented way. "It's taken a long time, huh? They were well-rewarded. I hope we get a lot more games on national television, on the big networks, not just your sports networks. ABC, I think, really lucked out today."

Over the summer there was some player movement but dramatically less than one might expect for an Iowa team that had become completely Clark's team. The top seven players in minutes from Clark's freshman year stayed for her sophomore season, and while a pair of teammates, Lauren Jensen and Megan Meyer, transferred to Creighton and Drake, respectively, Iowa added Kylie Feuerbach to the mix. In both cases Clark and her teammates couldn't be more effusive about the two departing players. Clark kept in touch with Meyer, and the whole team, especially Martin, gushed about Jensen ahead of Iowa facing Creighton in the NCAA Tournament. Feurbach decided to transfer from Iowa State to Iowa, the college basketball equivalent of leaving the Montagues for the Capulets. And she did it with her eyes wide open about what it would mean to play with Clark. She'd been her teammate for two years of high school AAU ball with the All-Iowa Attack. "She made a great decision to come here," Clark said in July 2021. "She wants to win, and that's what we want to do." The stability of players around Clark bought into what Bluder, Jan Jensen, and Jenni Fitzgerald were preaching and would prove critical to Iowa's growth and success.

Bluder had told me that she'd have given her Hawkeyes an F for defense after Clark's freshman year. She said that if they could get to a C+, "we have the opportunity to do some special things." That defensive rating jumped from 338th in the country to 216th, hardly world-class but plenty good enough to make the top-rated offensive team in the country a threat to win it all. Clark was part of that defensive improvement. "She just played really small defensively her freshman year. She played all hunched over with her arms down, and we got her to understand you've got to occupy space," Bluder said in July 2024. "And she just understood it so much better, even her sophomore year, about what was needed, but then I think she got better every year."

But if missing the Olympic team qualified as Clark's awakening in the 2024 WNBA season, the way her sophomore season ended counted as the collegiate version of it. The Hawkeyes found another level by Big Ten Tournament time, crushing Northwestern and Nebraska before beating a terrific Indiana team despite future Fever teammate Grace Berger matching Clark shot for shot. The Hawkeyes were seeded second in the Greensboro region and were a popular dark horse pick to win it all. Instead, after routing Illinois State in front of a sold-out Carver-Hawkeye Arena in Round One, their shocked fans saw Lauren Jensen herself knock down the game-winning three to send Iowa out of the tournament short of even the Sweet 16 they'd reached the year before.

Everything had been set up. Iowa got the ABC game because the networks learned from 2021. (Ultimately, 993,000 would watch the Round of 32 game.) And Carver-Hawkeye was entirely sold out all weekend. Bluder, as she always did, took the high road in her opening statement. "Obviously, just want to congratulate Creighton. A very well-played game, executed really well, defended really well. That's a hard matchup for us. Five guards is a hard matchup. We knew that," she said. "But they did a great job, and Lauren Jensen was here last year. Obviously, that's an incredible storyline. She goes over there and she comes back and beats us on our home court, and I want to congratulate her because she's a great kid. She is a really, really good kid. I'm happy for her. I wish it wasn't in this situation, but I am happy for her that she's found a really good home and is really having a lot of success. Our crowd today was amazing again. I think we broke the NCAA record for first and second rounds of attendance, and I apologize to our fans that they couldn't celebrate a victory with us today."

How many coaches have you heard speak about a player who transferred from their program like that—let alone just after she ended the season of her former team? That is not to say it didn't sting. "We were playing really well at the end of the year, and that's what made that loss to Creighton so tough," Bluder said in July 2024. "What made that so tough was because we had scrimmaged Creighton earlier in the year in that closed scrimmage and beaten them…. One of our players that transferred was now starting for

Creighton, Lauren Jensen, and she hit the game-winner. So there's just so many things that just made it like salt in the wound, right? But I did think, looking back on it, *Damn it would have been great to have gone to a Sweet 16.* We would have faced Iowa State, who we'd already beaten that year. But it made everybody really, really driven that summer."

And for her part, Clark was already able to put it into broader perspective just minutes after her sophomore season ended. "Obviously a wonderful opportunity for a women's basketball game today on ABC in front of a sold-out crowd," Clark said to assembled reporters from the podium. "I just feel bad for the fans because they've given us so much over these past two weeks, really willed us to a regular-season title here at home versus Michigan, and I hope they come out and support us the exact same way next year. I know they will."

Iowa finished fifth in the nation in attendance at 8,221 per game, but it is worth noting that both Bluder and Clark were still urging them to return. Neither one had fully internalized yet the given that an audience for Clark had become. "There's a lot of exciting basketball ahead for this group, but obviously the feeling of letting them down, letting the coaches down, our teammates down, it stinks right now," Clark said. "But I think overall just more fuel for us going into next year."

With the benefit of hindsight, that's how Bluder saw it, too, though not at first. "I hate losing, and so does she, so much," Bluder said the following July.

But Caitlin's brother, Blake, would send his sister the picture of that scoreboard from the Creighton game repeatedly through her junior season. It spurred Clark—and Iowa as well—to even greater heights. They were inseparable now. The legend grew from the inside out. First Clark would show off an ability no one had ever seen before—but in practice, including a late-October scrimmage at the dawn of her sophomore year where she hit five threes in a row—and then she'd do it in a game, as when she nearly brought Iowa back from a 25-point deficit at Michigan later that season, and the world would see what her coaches already knew.

This manifested itself in things like a game-winning shot in front of a sold-out Carver-Hawkeye Arena to beat Indiana, then ranked second in the country, near the end of Clark's junior season. But it also would show up in plays like she made near the end of a closely fought contest at Rutgers in February of her sophomore year. With the game still in the balance with 30 seconds left, Clark secured a defensive rebound and somehow knew her teammate, McKenna Warnock, was streaking down the court more than 70 feet away. Not only did Clark have the presence of mind to find her teammate, but she also managed to heave the ball backward, over her head, directly into Warnock's hands for the touchdown pass, and Warnock finished the play with a layup to put the game out of reach. "She impacts the game in so many different ways.... People sometimes just get fixated on that scoring, where it's other things as well," Bluder told me after that 87–78 win at the Rutgers Athletic Center. "And you're right, that pass—well, I'm saying McKenna should be a center fielder because that was an unbelievable catch, great hands, and McKenna converted it."

Clark, just listening next to her coach, nodded, smiling: "That was beautiful. I mean, it put us up double possessions." Clark had five steals that night, too, playing "longer," as she explained it to me postgame. "I always like to be thinking a step ahead."

That was the essence of the Clark experience. It's not only about the show itself or the artist performing, but also doing so in the service of winning.

The evening's media event ended with Bluder respectfully but forcefully making the case for Clark as player of the year, just as Dawn Staley was for her star, Aliyah Boston. The two would meet again.

By her junior year, this duality in Clark's game—magic in the service of winning—would reveal itself to a larger audience than any women's basketball player had ever experienced.

Remembering Bluder's comment about the C+ grade, I asked her what the new goals were for her Hawkeyes as Clark's junior year began in October of 2022. "We made a huge jump," she said. "We went up like 100 spots in synergy from two years ago to last year's season. But there's work to be done still, and that's what's exciting. We do have one of the top offensive teams in the country, but if we can, let's try to get to a B- this year, and let's try to also work on our rebounding. We can get more offensive and defensive rebounds is another area that we're really trying to stress with our program this year. And so, boy, I think if we can improve in both of those areas, we could be fighting for another championship."

The Hawkeyes became particularly proficient at ending possessions of opponents with defensive rebounds—something Bluder pointed out was not only a defensive skill, but also one in which Clark excelled at as a guard—rising from 236th in the country as a team during Clark's freshman year to 109th her sophomore season to 30th her junior campaign. That was particularly frightening for opponents because defensive rebounds grabbed by Clark also served as a labor-saving device for her team, who'd look to get the ball into her hands to begin any offensive possession anyway and increased the chances of an Iowa transition opportunity, where the Hawkeyes excelled beyond any other team in efficiency with an absurd 1.23 points per possession in transition Clark's junior year.

This was generally considered Clark's best chance to win a title. Czinano, the resident Jan Jensen-infused hyper-efficient big for the Hawkeyes, returned for 2022–23 season but would be out of eligibility after that. "Coach Jensen does such a great job," Bluder said in October 2022. "She's our associate head coach, and we've coached together for 30 years now, along with Jenni Fitzgerald, and I'm so blessed to have that consistency in my coaching staff. Jan has our post players, and I just think she does such a great job of footwork and ceiling and getting them to understand they don't need to dribble the basketball. Read the defense, have the position before you catch the ball, and then just shoot the ball. It's not that complicated. But I think people try to overcomplicate post play. Sometimes I think they think they need to have nine moves that I can go to when I'm doing my post moves. Well, how about just four basic moves? Why not just have four basic moves and do the same old boring thing really well over and over and over again? I don't mind that."

The continuity up and down the roster meant a team more connected defensively and capable of knowing precisely where each of them would be at any given moment. That was a particularly useful skillset around the most precise passer in the history of the sport. Clark's assist percentage reflected this. As a freshman it was 40.1 percent, ranking a remarkable eighth in the country among all players. As a sophomore it reached 43.3 percent for third in the nation. But as a junior, it climbed to 49.5 percent, a level rarely seen in the modern era, especially considering her turnover percentage kept dropping in the process. As a senior it was a whopping 51.6 percent. It may not be a mark anyone ever touches. More than half the time when an assist was possible, Clark found it and had her teammate convert the opportunity.

Word was getting around. Iowa had historically traveled well as a fanbase, but there were even more Hawkeyes fans than usual at the Rutgers Athletic Center when Iowa visited in February of Clark's sophomore year. By the dawn of her junior season, Bluder had a vision for what it might look like. "Last year when we filled Carver the last three games of the year. That kind of felt like we have taken this to a different level," Bluder said, echoing the precise vision C. Vivian Stringer had when she took over the Iowa program 40 years before. "When you come into a program, you walk into Carver the first time, and you see all those seats. *Man, I would love to fill this place. Wouldn't it be fun to fill this place?* And then to have it happen three times in a row—and not just once but three times in a row—was really fulfilling."

Bluder also noted how often Clark would greet fans on the road, such as the moment a young girl asked Clark for her shoelaces at a game in Nebraska. "After the game Caitlin went over and not only gave her shoelaces, but gave her both shoes," Bluder said. "The women are so good in our game at speaking to the next level and being role models and being great ambassadors of our game. And Caitlin made that girl cry. She might have been a Cornhusker going into that arena, but she was an Iowa Hawkeye fan coming out of it."

Clark and the Iowa team made Hawkeyes fans of so many people in the 2022–23 season. The 2022 WNBA Finals averaged 555,000 viewers per game. A few weeks later, an early-season non-conference matchup between Iowa and UConn on ABC drew 597,000 even without Bueckers, who UConn had lost for the season due to injury. By December 588,000 tuned into the CyHawk Classic. That's roughly as many as had tuned into the ABC contest, even though it aired on ESPN2. Iowa–Indiana, a game between the Big Ten regular-season champion Hoosiers and the eventual tournament title winner Hawkeyes, drew 622,000 viewers. And when Clark came around a Czinano screen to sink a buzzer-beating three, it elevated the sound from more than 15,000 people in Carver-Hawkeye Arena to a level no one there had ever heard before. The clip replayed endlessly as an advertisement for March Madness, which finally would be the branding the women could use as well as the men, thanks to the ever-so-late change by the NCAA. "I've shot a lot of those, whether it was with my two brothers in the driveway, a lot by myself," Clark said after the game. "I'm lucky enough to have done it for my team in front of 15,000 people who wanted to scream about it."

And then came the postseason.

No one could come close to matching up with Iowa at the Big Ten Tournament played at the Target Center, where back in 2015 a young Clark witnessed her first live WNBA game between the Minnesota Lynx and Indiana Fever, in early March. "I want to say I was in…fifth grade, so however old you are then, but it was my first-ever WNBA game," Clark remembered in July 2024. "I remember being at the hotel, and I was swimming in the pool, and my dad called the ticket office to get tickets to the game because we drove up here and didn't have any. And the guy that was working at the ticket office was like, 'Does she want to come and watch shootaround?' … And I remember I got to sit court-side and watch all of that. So whoever that guy was: you're a hero, you're heaven-sent in my life…. But I remember Lindsay Whalen came over, Seimone Augustus came over. I remember meeting them very vividly. So obviously, a special memory in my entire basketball career."

That was the court she commanded in early March of 2023 when Iowa ran past Purdue 69–58, defeated Maryland 89–84 to avenge a late-February loss, and then demolished Ohio State 105–72. Clark posted a triple-double of 30 points, 17 assists, 10 rebounds—video game numbers—while winning a Big Ten title. And she had just two turnovers as well against Ohio State's vaunted pressure defense, which forced 20.1 turnovers a game to rank 14th in the country. It was as close to a perfect game as anyone had ever played in a Big Ten title contest. In a league with six top 25 teams to begin the year, Iowa walked away with the crown. And in a league filled with passionate fanbases, the entire arena rose to meet the moment Clark tracked down her 10th rebound on a long carom she knew she needed for the triple-double because Bluder told her so. "It was a fun moment with the arena," said Clark, sitting at the podium just after beating Ohio State that afternoon. "I started laughing a little bit. Our fans have been incredible. Our three games here, I don't know if we do it without them. It's really a home-court advantage. There's chanting 'Let's go Hawks' with 45 minutes left in warmups. That's probably pretty intimidating if I'm the other team. A lot of credit goes to them. They're incredible. It's been like that all season long. So we're just really thankful."

Iowa drew a No. 2 seed in the Seattle region and really wasn't contested for the duration of its run to a Final Four destiny Clark had spoken into existence the day she officially signed to come to University of Iowa, though that objective was doubted by many. Iowa's first- and second-round games sold out in 53 minutes. Their second-round win against Georgia drew 1.45 million television viewers. She set records for television viewing in each successive round. As the attention built, so did her performances.

Louisville just had absolutely no answer for her in the regional final. Clark rose to the occasion with perhaps her best game at Iowa. She scored 41 points and grabbed 10 rebounds, and every one of her teammates elevated alongside her. The quintet of Clark, Czinano, Warnock, Martin, and Gabbie Marshall had 90 starts together as of the Louisville game. They played as one unit. Clark had 12 assists, and the group made a season-high 16 threes. It was the 11th triple-double of Clark's career. And no one had ever scored 30 points in an NCAA Tournament triple-double game—let alone 40.

When Bluder substituted Clark out of the game, the smile Clark allowed herself stood in sharp contrast to the neutral face she presents to the world most of the time she's on the court, and she allowed herself, too, a wave to the crowd before her coach got a huge bear hug as she jogged off the court, as the outcome was no longer in doubt with 22 seconds left. When it was over, she carried the regional trophy around over her head, showing it to the thousands of yellow-and-black-clad Hawkeyes fans who'd made the trip out west.

This is what it meant to be Clark in 2023.

And just minutes after playing the game at a level equal to anyone who's ever done it, she displayed her ability to see the bigger picture. "When I'm playing my best basketball is when I'm playing, when I'm having the most fun out of anybody on court," she said. "I love to play this game. I've dreamed of this moment since I was a little girl. I've always wanted to take a team to the Final Four and be in these moments and have confetti fall down on me. But I play this game because I love it, and it brings joy to me, and it brings a lot of joy to other people because our team is so fun to watch. I don't play it to hoist a trophy, whether it's individually or with my team. That just comes with the joy and the passion that we play for and how much fun we have with one another. So, yeah, I think it's just who I am. At the end of the day, I'm a fun person off the court, too, maybe a little too goofy at times. But I think that's what makes basketball so fun for me."

The three elements that serve as separators for Clark were all clearly identifiable in the signature victory of her college career—the national semifinal win against South Carolina at the 2023 Final Four in Dallas. Yes, there was the shooting, a repeat of the 41 points from the Louisville game. She made the first shot of the night to serve notice that despite the Gamecocks entering the game as heavy favorites Iowa would not play from behind, something an excited Clark noted to punctuate Bluder's postgame speech in the locker room that night. There were the eight assists somehow on a night the shots weren't really falling for her teammates, South Carolina closed off the three-point spigot the Hawkeyes had relied on all year, and the nation's best defensive team limited touches to Czinano inside. Yet Clark supplemented her scoring with plays she managed to make amid Staley's flawless defensive gameplan.

But that third element—belief. That is what might be the most Iowa facet of Clark's triumph of all. The Van Horne Hornettes, who were texting each other, weren't all that worried the night Clark ended South Carolina's winning streak, instead noting with approval each successful screen. Jubilation built as their messages pinged back and forth across the country. Molly Kazmer's hands were sweating as she sat with them clasped in the stands at American Airlines Arena, watching Clark, feeling each shot as if it was her own but never wondering if she could pull it off.

In those final moments of the win against South Carolina, Clark threw the ball into the air, ran to the Iowa fans, and signaled to her ear. And, yes, everybody could hear her now. A team built by Staley with her assistant Jolette Law—who played for C. Vivian Stringer at Iowa—led her recruiting efforts in building a roster that includes at least seven players who will be drafted or play in the WNBA. And that juggernaut lost for what would turn out to be the only time in 75 games over two seasons.

The past and the present are so intertwined. Law felt it was bittersweet in 2023, when her South Carolina team lost to Clark and the Hawkeyes and bittersweet when she beat them in 2024. She remembered what she told Clark after she hugged her in the handshake line following both games. "When I hugged her the first time, it was, 'Go win it,'" Law said in a September phone interview. "The second time it was: 'Go keep being great.' People were like, 'How did you just hug Caitlin? She almost beat you. She beat you last year.' I want her to be great because she's a part of me. She's a part of the Iowa foundation that helped me, and wherever she goes, people can say, 'Oh, I don't like Caitlin Clark'. I'm like, 'I respect her. She's carrying the torch.' And it is all because of Coach Stringer."

It was the evolution from the women's basketball players who either needed to fight for attention or continually justify receiving it, the Laws and the Staleys, the Bluders and the Jensens, to the Caitlin Clark Generation, who never doubt for a moment that they belong and, as the building fills to capacity, smile at the idea some people are just now arriving. As Clark put it after her senior year: "I don't really get offended when people say, 'I never watched women's basketball before.' I think, *One, you're a little late to the party, yes, but, two, that's cool.* We're changing the game. We're attracting more people to it."

The Iowa–South Carolina semifinal had 5.6 million viewers on television alone. In the eye of the hurricane, Clark grew intensified with every shot. She still hadn't reckoned with the impact the night Iowa beat South Carolina. "Honestly, I don't think it's really hit me yet," she told me. "I don't think it will hit me for a couple more weeks. I'm trying to enjoy every single second of this. I will say what I really loved is I saw so many videos of people back in Iowa City, just every single bar completely packed, screaming about women's basketball. That's so, so cool to see your impact on your university and your state."

Word traveled fast about the show Clark and Iowa put on. For the title game between Iowa and LSU, 9.9 million watched on television. And despite the most attention ever paid to a women's basketball player, despite an uncharacteristic level of LSU three-point shooting to aid Reese's tremendous title game performance, which led to a 102–85 Iowa loss despite 30 points and eight assists from Clark, despite officiating that led to 37 foul calls and grinding the flow of the game to an absolute halt, despite Reese taking Clark's signature "you can't see me" gesture and directing it back at her in the waning moments of the title game, Clark never lost her composure. "Teach me," she'd told Bluder and Jensen, and the lessons took. LSU made more than nine threes just three times all season entering the game, but the Tigers hit seven of their first 10 in the first half. It was too much for Iowa to overcome. The defensive gameplan that encouraged LSU to take long-distance shots was practical but on that day unworkable.

The NCAA, meanwhile, could learn the lesson the Iowa Girls High School Athletic Union understood decades ago and invest some more of its budget on officiating. "I understand things aren't going to go my way," Clark said that weekend in Dallas. "I think accepting that, and that's not always something I've had throughout my college career. When I haven't gotten fouls called, when I've had turnovers, when I've had missed shots, it's kind of thrown me off my game a little bit. I think the physicality is something I've just come to accept at this point in my career. People are holding me, I have scratches, I have bruises, but so does everybody else. You can't complain. At this point of the season, refs aren't going to call it, nor could they down the court. I think it's just come with my mental toughness and working on that and accepting things aren't going to go your way. That's the game of basketball. All you've got to do is respond, and that's what's going to be best for your team."

Dressed impeccably as always in her black blazer and holding court just outside of the Iowa locker room that night, Jensen said: "It's just like you're raising a kid. I don't know if you guys are parents, but you have a toddler, sometimes you just say, 'No, no, no.' And you think they finally got it, and then—back in timeout, you know? And that's just kind of the process, but she's just done a beautiful job this year."

At that moment her niece, the indispensable Martin, walked by and shouted, "Love you, Coach Jan!" With a huge smile, Jensen interrupted her answer and answered, "Love you, Kate Martin! Enjoy it!"

It all felt like an apex because no one had ever reached these heights, but Clark was being asked to do it again in her senior season without Warnock and Czinano. The tears on the podium shed by everyone, including Clark, were focused on what had ended that day in Dallas. "Monika is one of the most fun people to be around," Clark said through her tears. "She's goofy, and she deserved a little better than that. Monika would tell you when she first got here she never dreamed to be as good as she is, and I still don't think she realizes how good she is, and other people don't realize it either. She doesn't get the credit she deserves. I told her after the game, 'I'm nothing without you.' She's made me a better person, a better basketball player, and I'm just really lucky that I was able to play with Mon and share a lot of really fun moments with her. I think we're one of the best post/guard duos to play the game, and I'm just really lucky and grateful to have had these years together."

Clark made it clear that day she expected to be back. And Czinano, from Watertown, Minnesota, a state with a potent legacy of women's basketball as well, gave a very Clark answer when she was asked about the newcomers to watching her sport. "Buckle up. I mean, it's only going to get more exciting and more fun," she said. "The game is evolving in such a great way. I'm glad you're tuning in now, but keep it up."

Then the team headed to a nearby bar and drank together into the night, unwilling to let that feeling of family, as Czinano put it, disappear. That, as much as any victory on the court, was Clark's reward for her evolution, her accepting the level her teammates could meet her at.

Clark didn't really have an offseason. Ad shoot after ad shoot beckoned. She showed up throughout the offseason for Iowa, the WNBA campaign as ever-present as any of the already-professional players. The Hawkeyes took a summer trip to Croatia and Italy together. Mobbed by fans, she played in the John Deere Classic Pro-Am in Silvis. (If Clark has ever refused an autograph request, no record could be found.) Sitting at the podium after her admittedly uneven round of golf next to Zach Johnson, it was the PGA Tour pro and Iowa native who gushed about Clark, calling her "transcendent." The natural order of things as accepted all over the country for so long with men's sports atop women's sports did not hold in Iowa.

The sequel, somehow, didn't just live up to the original. It exceeded it in virtually every measure. It was a very big deal when Stringer sold out Carver-Hawkeye Arena on February 3, 1985. When Iowa sold out three games in a row in 2022–23, it resonated with Bluder, who made note of it at a press conference.

Iowa's entire 2023–24 home slate was sold out by August 2. Both Bluder and Jensen, who heard the news together, started crying. By October the season had unofficially begun. To watch the Iowa women's basketball team face DePaul in an exhibition game, 55,646 people poured into Kinnick Stadium—not Carver-Hawkeye Arena. It was Bluder's idea and a tribute as much to Stringer and Christine Grant as it was to the current Iowa team. "I go meet with our athletic director—Beth

Goetz—and said, 'I have this idea,'" Bluder said in July 2024. "We want to break the attendance record for women's basketball. Let's have a game in Kinnick Stadium, and I'd love it if 50,000 people came to this game, and Beth didn't blink. She just was like, 'Yeah, that's a great idea.' And a lot of ADs would have thought of all the reasons not to do it, and she thought of all the reasons why it was the right time."

The game raised $250,000 for Iowa Stead Children's Family Hospital, which has a direct sightline into the stadium. Clark, Bluder, and all of Iowa, it felt like, waved to the children after the first quarter. The entire afternoon felt to Bluder like an affirmation of her life's work. "There were women in the stands crying with emotion that this was happening for women," she said. "And it was such a moment for women's athletics to see that happen. People say, 'What are some of your happiest moments or proudest moments?' That's one of them, having that crossover in Kinnick and the impact it had on other people and the excitement it generated."

But she also noted, pointedly—it made the season even longer. And no one ever experienced a season quite like Iowa and Clark did in 2023–24. Iowa was without Czinano or Warnock, but Clark and Bluder convinced Martin and Marshall to return, and both proved pivotal to the success of the Hawkeyes in pursuit of another Final Four appearance.

The joy Clark took in the decisions of her two close friends to return was evident when she laid out how she did it in October 2023. "Yeah, I would say I definitely tried to persuade them," Clark said from the Big Ten Media Day podium. "Obviously, they're two of my best friends. Gabbie to me was a little bit more of a lock to come back. Kate, not so much. But Kate was probably just trying to be dramatic and wanted me to beg her so she felt better about herself. I'm kidding, but, yeah, I think the biggest thing is Kate is a really, really good leader and is somebody that you want on your team no matter what sport it is, no matter what age group it is, no matter male or female, she will just lead. That's the type of person she is. She attracts people to follow her, one of the best teammates I've ever been around.

"Then obviously Gabbie, one of the best shooters, but I don't think she gets enough credit for her defense. I told her she needs to be Defensive Player of the Year, and then she's like, 'Nah, Caitlin, that's for you. It's your last one to get.' And I just started laughing. So we joke about that now. But no...she takes the challenge of guarding the best player every single game. And the South Carolina game, for example, she doesn't score a single point, maybe shoots the ball one, two, three times—I don't even remember exactly—but she defended every single possession, and I think she played 38 minutes. That's just the type of player and teammate that

Gabbie is. She's going to give her all. She's not going to hang her head if she doesn't get her opportunities on offense, but she's going to give everything she has on defense. At the same time, I think that needs to change this year. We have to find ways to get Gabbie the ball and get her shots because she's one of the best shooters I've ever seen, as we all saw at the end of the season. Kate, too, I think they both are going to have to take a step forward on offense and take a little bit more of a prominent role because we lose two people that gave us a lot on that side of the ball."

Within this answer held one of the biggest on-court challenges for Clark, Bluder, and Jensen in what turned out to be their last ride together. For much of the preceding decade, the Iowa women's basketball team deployed, in addition to an elite point guard, the honorary Jensen center, utilizing Bethany Doolittle, then Gustafson, then Czinano as the platonic ideal of footwork; Mikan-Drills-turned-layups; and the resulting hyper efficiency to play alongside an elite point guard (Logic, then Kathleen Doyle, then Clark) and what is immediately recognizable as the third prong of the old six-on-six offense, where shooters support those two figures to help spread the floor.

The shooters were back, Clark was back, but Czinano was gone, and it was up to Jensen and Bluder to figure out what the center position would look like. Addison O'Grady,

Sharon Goodman, and A.J. Ediger were the three bigs on hand. Hannah Stuelke entered the season as a power forward. It would be up to Clark to maximize them and for Bluder and Jensen to figure out how to make them viable enough targets to keep Clark as effective a creator and distributor as she'd been through the first three years. "Yeah, I think it's definitely a work in progress," Clark said when asked about this point in October. "I don't think it can really be put into words how different it is to have a post and a guard combo that get three years to play with each other. If you watched me and Monika our first year, there were quite a few miscues, and she wouldn't always slide to where I wanted her. She would get hit in the face with the ball, she wouldn't know if it's coming. I think it's just a work in progress. I think the biggest thing for me that I'm trying to live by is just instilling confidence in them. They understand how great Monika was, but they don't need to be Monika. That's something we always talk about is they're going to be different. They shouldn't be expected to be Monika. They can do things that Monika couldn't and they can't do some things that Monika could. They're just different.

"But they bring a lot of really good things to this team, and I think that's the biggest thing for myself as a point guard is you just have to continue to give them the ball. If they make a mistake, if they turn it over, whatever it is, take the blame but continue to give them the ball because we need our posts to be really successful, and I honestly think all three of our posts, Sharon, A.J., and Addie, have been really good. And Hannah plays there at times. So they're competing every day in practice, and that's all you would want."

If there was a lesson out of Clark's senior season on the court, it was this: she simply made everyone better around her. She elevated her points per possession on the pick-and-roll north of a point per possession for the first time in her collegiate career, while her assist percentage soared north of 50 percent. And Stuelke, who became the de facto starter at the post, along with Goodman and Ediger, topped 60 percent shooting from the field.

None of that was preordained, and it required more of Clark—notably patience with her teammates. It helped her grow as a leader. And it even prepared her for the process of learning how to play as a rookie with Boston, a generational talent in her own right but not someone who operated out of the pick-and-roll regularly in her time starring at South Carolina.

Off the court, the Caitlin Clark Effect kept rewriting the audience expectations for not only Iowa games, but also women's basketball as a whole. On January 13 when FOX aired Iowa–Indiana on its main network as part of Saturday

Night Hoops—originally a men's basketball timeslot—more than a million people watched. So the following Sunday, NBC joined the fun, flexing its game into the primary network for a Sunday afternoon, January 21, Iowa at Ohio State game, and 1.86 million tuned in. That topped every single men's college hoops broadcast that week by at least 50 percent. And Clark scored 45 points in that one despite a rare loss for Iowa in 2023–24.

Another 1.7 million watched Iowa–Nebraska on Super Bowl Sunday on FOX, while Clark's March 3, 2024, game against Ohio State at sold-out Carver-Hawkeye Arena—39 years after Stringer filled it for the first time for a women's game, also against Ohio State—drew 3.38 million viewers, more than double any other college basketball game. The traveling Caitlin Clark Show had turned into the kind of spectacle usually reserved for The Beatles or Taylor Swift.

At Maryland in early February, word spread that the Hawkeyes would be descending an escalator to board the team bus in College Park at the team's hotel, riding a few blocks away to the XFINITY Center. Dozens, then hundreds, massed around the roped-off escalator, resulting in thunderous ovations for anyone wearing black and/or gold. Even the equipment managers got applause and cheers and then sheepishly waved to the crowd. Fans had gathered with signs, and it was possible to see each of the Iowa players register with surprise that this was their life now as they descended down an escalator, producing cheers and adoration among the following crowds. Bluder, though, was all in. She stopped to greet fans in the front of the crowd, high-fiving everyone as she reveled in the moment. She'd been at women's basketball's quiet beginning and wasn't about to miss a moment of this new high. After all, tickets had cost fans more than $1,000 on the secondary market. "This is a circus," Jensen said, remembering it all in the summer of 2024. "I mean that in a good way, right? But we talked about it like when the circus comes to town. It was so fun. When you read the books where—of course, none of us are *that* old—but it's like, everybody's watching the tent set up, and the exotic elephant is there. Well, that was everywhere we would go. I mean, no normal person gets to have a rope, right? I mean, we have ropes all the time."

Finally, Clark herself, a composed smile, knowing this wasn't just her life at Iowa but for the foreseeable future, took it all in as she descended the escalator. Every effort was simultaneously designed to navigate the moment and save strength for all that would be expected of her. And even when the Iowa bus disappeared, the fans stayed in the hotel lobby, congregating, not wanting any moment of the greatest season any of them had ever experienced to end. "I take it in everywhere I go, and I think I'm just very grateful, and obviously it's changed my life in some ways more than others, just being more aware of my surroundings," Clark said when asked about the latest sellout crowd she thrilled. "People spend a lot of time, money, and resources to come see us play, and whenever I step on the court, I just want to have a lot of fun. And I've been able to find a lot of joy and calmness in that."

The tables had turned in the Iowa–Maryland matchup from Clark's freshman season. It was the Hawkeyes who entered with experience, while a young Brenda Frese-led Maryland team was still learning to play together. Iowa expertly navigated the challenge. Clark scored 38, and her seven threes thrilled the many Iowa fans within a sellout crowd at XFINITY, which contained plenty of Maryland faithful as well, in a 93–85 Hawkeyes victory. It was Bluder's first win at XFINITY Center, something she noted as she sat down with us in a packed media room for postgame.

Stuelke and O'Grady combined for 15 points. There was connection between the bigs and Clark that appeared to be reaching a new level, something Clark confirmed when I asked her about it that night. "So 15 points out of the five position is pretty good," Clark said, scanning the box score in front of her as she answered me while Bluder nodded next to her on the podium. "I still think we can get them involved a little bit more. I think, especially Hannah, get her a few more easier looks…. It's different. We're running two people in and out [of the post], but I thought they were physical. I thought they were strong. They only shoot 14 shots. So it's not really that many. They're both 50 percent from the field and 15 points, so I still think there's ways we can get them all the more involved and be a little stronger and set them up for some better looks."

Clark saw it first. Five days later, Stuelke scored 47 points against Penn State, going 17-for-20 from the field. Clark's 15 assists tied her season high. Even at this late stage of her college career, Clark still recognized ways to get better and incorporated them into her game almost seamlessly. And Molly Davis, who'd paid her dues, was establishing herself as a legitimate scorer behind Clark and Martin. It seemed Iowa had figured out the playbook for the rest of Clark's senior season. But Davis tore a ligament in her knee against Ohio State on March 3, and it was left to Bluder, Jensen, Fitzgerald, and Clark to cobble together a new plan for the final stretch run of Clark's Iowa career. Even as the group descended every escalator to massive attention, they innovated in real time within the brightest spotlight.

Somehow, despite all of this on-court turmoil—not to mention a defense that essentially stalled out at the C+ Bluder wanted from Clark's sophomore year—the Hawkeyes got better, and it happened on the offensive end. Their offensive rating of 117.4 in Clark's senior year would be the highest mark of her four seasons at Iowa. The Hawkeyes captured another Big Ten Tournament title with routs of Penn State and Michigan, followed by an overtime classic win against Nebraska that required every one of Stuelke's 25 points, as Sydney Affolter stepped up to assume Davis' role. Iowa earned that one seed, beat Holy Cross easily and West Virginia with some difficulty in front of adoring, sell-out crowds at Carver-Hawkeye Arena. (It was no longer worth noting when the Hawkeyes sold out. It would have been a story at this point if it wasn't.) Clark was her customary self in postgame, breaking down the ways she could have played better, grateful she got to play on. And then, it appeared to hit her—the ending she'd authored. "I can't believe I'm a senior," she said, "and I just played my last game here."

From there it was onto Albany and looming in the distance was a chance to avenge last season's national title loss in an Elite Eight game against LSU. First, Iowa needed to beat five-seeded Colorado. A fan behind me, sitting in her de rigueur Clark 22 black jersey asked her mom: "When does Iowa come out?"

Oh, you'll know. The collective shriek is louder than any to come before it in women's basketball. Just after the previous game between UCLA and LSU had even ended, an army of young women in 22 shirts descended the stairs, trying to get just a glimpse as Clark ran out of the tunnel with her teammates. She grabbed the ball, expressionless, and went over to her basket to begin her work. In the arena it was their first live look at Clark. For Clark, it was simply Saturday.

Clark quietly worked her way around the perimeter, getting her shot up in no particular hurry. This could've been her last game in the Iowa uniform as she played for a chance to earn redemption—against LSU, a return to the Final Four, a chance to take that final step and win it all—but at no point did this pressure coerce her into doing things any differently. She had internalized all the pressure and found that treating every day—the way a great shooter treats every shot the same—is vital to guide her through this historic run, as if she was any other player, as if this was any other game. It's the way she's learned to lock in. She was there to work.

Clark took one final free throw, followed by one final long three, and then was satisfied. Clapping her hands three times and watching the balls of her teammates go into the hoop, Clark rebounded for them. A few minutes later, the shrieks, as the lineups were announced, astounded many in the building, though no one in black and gold was surprised anymore. "Honestly, I think when I step on the court, a calming sense comes over me," Clark told me. "This is where I'm supposed to be. I have 13 amazing teammates that have my back. These are the moments you've worked so hard for. This is what you've put the time in for, in the gym all by yourself, and with your teammates. I guess it's just kind of like go let your work shine, go have fun, go have a blast, and win or lose, there's a lot to hold your head high about. I thought that's exactly what we did. Everybody kind of played with a smile on their face and had a lot of fun."

"Good shot! Good shot!" said Bluder after a kickout to Clark led to a miss from deep. She knew there was only the next shot, the next pass, and no such thing as forcing because Clark could simply drift further away from the rim and give her teammates even more space to operate. Moments later, a laser beam from Clark to Affolter allowed the latter to streak to the basket without breaking stride. The pass hit her in the hands precisely as she began her motion up and in for a layup. Iowa extended its lead, and Colorado called timeout.

No longer was Iowa at the mercy of Clark's temper. She had become so frequently the calming presence for her team, as she was after a rushed possession, hands out to calm her teammates heading back to the bench for an officials' timeout. By the final minutes of the win against Colorado, Clark showed signs of knowing her work was done, treating the basketball like a soccer ball at one end, going behind her back once, then again probing the Colorado defense at the other end. Bluder, too, knew her night was done, subbing her out as the Albany crowd stood and cheered for her. Three games left.

At the final buzzer, mayhem prevailed. Hundreds gathered around the tunnels to scream for Clark, who signed as many signs and other materials as she could. Meanwhile, the screams were equally vociferous for Bluder and Marshall, who dutifully signed and high-fived the gathered crowd as well. Most of the signs were homemade.

Iowa dispatched Colorado easily in the Sweet 16, while the Tigers, the three seed in the Albany region, needed to mildly upset UCLA to reach the Elite Eight game. The year before 9.9 million people had watched LSU–Iowa in the national title game, and the audience peaked north of 12 million. This time the stakes were simply to return to the Final Four. Just how big would the numbers get? "Everybody is pretty excited for it," Bluder said. "Twelve million people tuned in last year to see this game, might be the same this time. Who knows? I know that these are two really good basketball teams, and it's almost unfortunate they're meeting this early. But everybody that's left now is really good. LSU is certainly that. Again, I haven't looked at our scout yet. I haven't gotten ready for that. But I just know it's going to be highly emotional and highly competitive."

In many ways the second Iowa–LSU game simply wasn't a rematch. The Hawkeyes were without Czinano and Warnock, while the Tigers had absolutely loaded up in the transfer portal, adding elite talents like Aneesah Morrow and Hailey Van Lith to Reese's relentless drive and talent in the middle. Flau'jae Johnson, too, had elevated her game above any of the perimeter players on LSU's title-winning team. This was a much tougher lift for Iowa.

It was fairly bewildering to Clark and Reese alike why there were any efforts to seed bad blood between them. Clark was always quick to point out the obvious—the two players didn't even guard one another. The ways each of them manifested themselves upon a basketball game differed so dramatically. And they'd even been teammates on multiple USA Basketball occasions. "I've been playing Caitlin since we were in high school," Reese said ahead of their rematch in Albany. "I played her in my AAU championship when she played for Iowa Attack, played her at Maryland, and then of course played her here at LSU, just a super competitive relationship, being able to play against each other and then last year at the national championship. Being able to just grow women's basketball and just being able to help the game is just something that we've just had."

Coming off the floor after warmups, Caitlin didn't smile until she had made eye contact with Bluder before giving her a high-five on her way into the tunnel. Jensen looked at Bluder and smiled. "She's ready," Jensen said with a smile. And then the lights went out. Intro time. Cue the shrieking.

The game absolutely lived up to the hype. Part of a 54–36 edge LSU held on the boards, Reese grabbed 20 rebounds and added 17 points. She twisted her ankle midway through the second quarter but just kept coming. Johnson scored 23 as LSU head coach Kim Mulkey chose to instead utilize Van Lith on Clark defensively to free up Johnson to score more. But Van Lith was utterly overmatched by Clark, also a longtime teammate of Van Lith's in USA Basketball. Clark scored 41 points to match her output in both the regional final and national semifinal the season before. In the final seconds, Clark dribbled out the clock, heaving the ball with purpose into the stands, right to her parents, while Bluder and Jensen embraced. "She's a great player," a resigned Van Lith said afterward of Clark. "She hit some tough shots. There's not a whole lot you can do about some of the threes she hit."

When it was over, the full scale of the complicated stardom of Clark in women's basketball was on display. As Reese explained, this is what it felt like to be publicly cast in the role of villain: "I don't really get to stand up for myself," she said through tears that night in Albany. "I mean, I have great teammates. I have a great support system. I've got my hometown. I've got my family that stands up for me. I don't really get to speak out on things because I just ignore. I just try to stand strong. I've been through so much. I've seen so much. I've been attacked so many times, death threats, I've been sexualized, I've been threatened, I've been so many things, and I've stood strong every single time…. I just want to always know, I'm still a human. All this has happened since I won the national championship…. And it sucks, but I still wouldn't change anything, and I would still sit here and say I'm unapologetically me."

Reese did not blame Clark any more than Clark blamed Reese for the complicated factors that turned stardom for women's basketball players into something far more fraught than it ever should have been for either one of them. In her next breath, Reese reiterated how much she knew that game had changed what everyone understood to be the ceiling for the sport's audience, and she was right: 12.3 million watched it, and the peak was 16 million. That number easily outperformed the 2023 NBA Finals television ratings.

And there were still two games to go for Clark and Iowa.

Among the many ways 2024 unfolded in ways that maximized both Clark's opportunities and the ability of women's basketball to grow as a result was the NCAA Tournament schedule. The rematch against LSU at the time was treated in part as coming too soon. Wouldn't the Final Four be anticlimactic? Well, not exactly.

The semifinal featured a chance for Clark and Iowa to face Bueckers and UConn. In normal times the two players would be facing one another with the same timelines, having both entered college for the 2020–21 season while commonly pitted against one another in arguments about who was better. But between Bueckers' injuries, Clark's endless rise in prominence, and Bueckers' decision to return for another collegiate season in 2024–25, this felt as much about passing a baton as anything else—one that could just have easily featured Clark vs. JuJu Watkins of USC, who'd fallen just short in the Elite Eight against UConn as a freshman. When people around the game point out that while Clark is extraordinary there are plenty of stars coming just behind her, they're not exaggerating.

For decades the complaint around women's college basketball was that UConn got too much attention. If anything, Bueckers had landed in a supplemental starring role to Clark on the national landscape, a rare thing for a Huskies star, which reflected the new, elevated ceiling for attention on the game. "She's done things this year that no one's ever done before," Coach Auriemma said of Bueckers the day before the national semifinal. "In the midst of all those great players, I saw a stat today that in the last 25 years, there's only two players that have averaged over 25 points, eight assists or whatever, eight rebounds, blocks, steals, and that's her and LeBron all across basketball. But she does it in a way that doesn't make everybody jump up and down, and she's old news."

How did the 11-time national champion plan to stop Clark? "We don't," he said. "We don't plan on stopping her because I tried calling all the other coaches that have stopped her, and none of them answer the phone. So we're going to have to find a different way to win than stopping Caitlin Clark."

They almost did—Clark and Bueckers played to a draw, and Aaliyah Edwards proved to be a difficult guard inside for Iowa's three-headed bigs. But Stuelke provided just what Iowa needed with 23 points, more than even Clark's 21, and the Hawkeyes returned to the national final.

In the wake of that win, Clark and Bluder even allowed themselves to think about what Iowa would look like when she was gone, responding to my question about what she and Stuelke had managed to develop over the season's final weeks. "Hannah's tremendous. I think it's just the confidence and belief. I think tonight she played with an energy about herself of she really could go in there and dominate," Clark said. "She goes toe to toe with Aaliyah Edwards, who in my mind is one of the best players in the country. It was physical with her, guarded her well, boxed her out. And she wasn't afraid to take it at her either, I thought. When they subbed in some post players off the bench, Hannah continued to go at them. And I'm just super happy for Hannah. She's worked so hard to be in this moment. She goes 5-for-7 from the free-throw line, made some big free throws for us. She was definitely a difference maker. I think this is the Hannah we all know, just having that confidence within herself because we all have it in her, just super happy for her."

Added Bluder: "We just kept telling her how good she was. Honestly, the only thing that stopped her from being great was her own self. It was her own doubt. And she is a beautiful athlete, an explosive athlete, and she just held herself back. And so we're trying to talk to her about positive self-talk instead of negative self-talk and kept pouring into her: 'You can do this. You can be such a beast if you want to be.' And so I'm just so pleased with her growth tonight. She just took as a sophomore—a young sophomore—she took another big leap tonight."

The shooting, the passing, the belief of Clark, it transcended her game and outlasted her at Iowa. Still, it wasn't quite enough to win it all. South Carolina lost only one time in 2022–23, and it came in the national semifinals to Iowa. That night Boston played her final game with the Gamecocks after a collegiate career that began with unfair comparisons to A'ja Wilson and ended with Boston's accomplishments so impressive they stacked up well against Wilson, who is immortalized with a statue on the South Carolina campus. Then Staley lost Boston to the WNBA Draft, one of five South Carolina players selected in the 2023 draft. She added several freshmen and transfers, notably Te-Hina Paopao, and her player development staff coached them all up. The recruiting was led by Law, who'd starred at point guard for Iowa under Stringer, who had first conceived of what Carver-Hawkeye could be. Law sometimes calls Dawn "Little Vivian."

In Clark's final game, South Carolina was simply too good. With a roster featuring subsequent 2024 lottery pick Kamilla Cardoso—who eight days later was selected by the Chicago Sky and paired with Reese—grabbing 17 rebounds, the bigger, taller Gamecocks outrebounded Iowa 51–29. Thirty points from Clark weren't nearly enough. The Gamecocks, retooled by Staley and Law, somehow just as effective defensively as they'd been, equally devastating in the paint even without Boston, were also capable of burying threes and hit eight from deep to nearly match Iowa's nine made threes.

South Carolina finished the season undefeated because the team had no weaknesses, something Clark acknowledged in the moments after her college career ended. "To be honest, after last year I was kind of like, *How do we top doing what we did last year?* Somehow, some way, every single person in our locker room believed. To be honest, this year was probably more special than last year," she said. "The teams we had to go through to get to this point, we won the Big Ten Tournament. We lost two players that were three-year starters for our program, and to be back in this position and come out here and battle—I mean, South Carolina is so good. There's only so much you can do. Cardoso has 17 rebounds. They have 51 as a team. We have 29. Hard to win a basketball game like that. You've basically got to shoot perfect at that point.

"I'm just proud of our group. We never backed down, and we gave it everything we've got."

In what turned out to be the last press conference she'd hold as Iowa head coach, Bluder didn't sound like someone with bitterness or regret, even though no one hates losing more than she does—not even Clark. She was asked about the accomplishment of reaching back-to-back finals. "It kind of makes me a double loser right now, quite honestly," she rejoined, flashing her wit in the moment of defeat. "It's tough. But I know how hard it is to get here, too. I say that tongue in cheek because I know it is really, really difficult to get to a Final Four. For us to be national runner-ups two years in a row, I'm never going to apologize. So many people last year—'Oh, you'll do it next time,' like it was terrible we didn't win the national championship. So many people said that to me. I'm like, 'Darn, you guys, we're national runner-ups. That's pretty good, too.' So I'm never going to apologize for finishing second in the country. But it sure would be nice to win one."

Staley paid tribute to Clark's impact, a mutual respect and understanding that both of them would continue to play a vital part in growing the game. And then she and Law called Coach Stringer to let her know they'd gotten another one, even though Stringer knew it already from watching it back at her home in New Jersey. But they wanted her to know that they'd gotten another one—and they'd gotten it for her.

For Iowa it was the end of an era, though anything but the end of Iowa basketball, as the millions, who had just discovered the phenomenon, failed to fully understand they'd uncovered a sport a century in the making. It was the last rodeo, too, for the trio who spent almost a quarter of that century molding that 20th century tradition into a 21st century. "Do not hang your heads," Bluder told her team, pulling herself together for one more team speech as Jensen stood nearby and nodded. "Do not. Yes, we're sad that the seniors are leaving us. It's tough. That's the tough part about this. But we got to do this together, right? We got to end this journey together. I'm proud of you all, you guys, so much. Each and every one of us. Do not hang your heads. Celebrate the fact that we were here. Celebrate that we got to do this together. All right, please, because that's what's important. You guys impacted so many people this year in a positive way. I mean, think of that, all the joy you brought to people, all the kids that you helped. That's what it's all about. Yes, you love a shiny trophy, but the impact that you had on young women in the sport doesn't get tarnished. It will always be there. You have raised this sport to a new level because of the way you play the game. Don't ever forget that."

The team huddled—shouted "Hawkeye Pride"—and then dispersed. The coaches hugged, too, and then it was finally just Jensen, sitting alone, a fitting precursor for the role she'd take on when Clark, then Bluder, moved on from the program. But Jensen wasn't alone. "The hug after in our staff locker room that night, and then I'm just sitting there and I was the last one out," Jensen told me a few months later. "I think that was the friend moment. Yeah, we were, we were part of it. It was a realization that that rocket ship will never go again. And it was sad, sure, but much more gratitude that I was in the ship because it was a ride."

CHAPTER SEVEN

The House That Vivian Built

C. Vivian Stringer was not the first head coach of the University of Iowa women's basketball team. She, though, was the first full-time coach, the first with a legitimate budget, and the first with a chance to implement a vision that few others even saw. But Iowa began playing varsity women's basketball in 1974–75, and to suggest that the Hawkeyes didn't begin to approach parity between that team and the men is an understatement. What was the proportion between the two budgets? Lark Birdsong, the first head coach at Iowa, explained: "If we had a penny, they had about a quadrillion of them."

Iowa women's basketball faced a multi-pronged financial problem in the early days, following the passage of Title IX in 1972. One was that the law did not simply wave a magic wand and create equal budgets for men's and women's sports. Iowa's force of nature in women's athletics, Christine Grant, told *The Des Moines Register* in September 1974 that her entire budget for women's athletics for the year totaled $70,000. Grant, then in her second year as Iowa's women's athletic director, also believed in the Association for Intercollegiate Athletics for Women (AIAW) model, which followed a different path from men's sports. Instead of funds being directed toward some of the most popular, money-making sports—as men's athletics did with football and basketball— Grant was a staunch believer in full equality between the women's sports. So while Drake went all in on women's basketball right away, hiring Carole Baumgarten and starting down the path of punching above its weight that continues today, things came slower for Iowa, which lost to Drake in its very first varsity game 75–64 before getting demolished by Bob Spencer's William Penn squad and then Molly Bolin's Grand View University.

Birdsong played three sports at University of Northern Colorado before enrolling at North Carolina to earn her master's degree in education with a physical education concentration. As with all the women who excelled in sports at this time, the dreams and limitations were a product of choices imposed by society rather than rising to meet the maximum level of their own abilities. "It was driven by what was available and what was inherently within me," Birdsong said of her path. "My dad once said to me when I was choosing my major, 'Would you want to come work in a business?' And I said, 'No, I can't see myself sitting at a desk all the days.' I was just wired for sports. I loved the camaraderie. I loved the physical pieces of it, the mental pieces of it. There was no other choice I could have made just because of who I was."

Grant heard about Birdsong and included her as part of her hires within the women's athletics department, which was entirely separate from the men's. Instead of being powered by gate receipts or even a separate budget, women's athletics came from a general university fund, which was part of why there were no full-ride scholarships for women's basketball players, just the opportunity to receive in-state tuition and potential work-study programs. "The concept of a major [revenue producing] and minor [non-revenue-producing] is incongruous to the philosophy and direction of our program," Birdsong said in a speech in 1976.

Of course, she understood what those limitations would mean for her basketball team. "I could see other schools that were getting scholarship money for their players and I could see them building up their basketball programs because they were getting more allocations than we were," Birdsong said in a September 2024 interview. "So we didn't have recruiting money. And if we did any recruiting, we paid for it out of our own pocket."

Even when circumstances produced opportunities, Iowa simply wasn't built to take advantage of them. The men's coach at the time, Lute Olsen, would sometimes scout women's players for Birdsong when he was on recruiting trips for the men, and he saw a post player, Inge Nissen, who he told Birdsong, "would come to Iowa if she'd give her a full ride." The rule, however, was the one scholarship needed to be divided four ways for women's basketball, just as with the other women's sports. "I went to Christine, and I explained why I wanted to have my one scholarship go to Inge, right? And she wouldn't let me," Birdsong said. "She just was so ingrained in her values, which is good, and because I'm a team player and I also value all the other sports, I said, 'Okay.'"

Nissen instead headed to Old Dominion University, won two national championships for Marianne Stanley, then headed to the WBL, and made the All-WBL team in 1981. She's in the Women's Basketball Hall of Fame now. She was 6'5" and certainly would have helped. The Hawkeyes finished their first season 5–16. In Season Two with all but one player a veteran of Iowa six-on-six girls basketball, they finished 9–19.

The reason was immediately apparent to Birdsong. "So the players that came in that were defensive players, it was difficult to teach them how to shoot in a short period of time," she recalled. "And so as I started to see what was coming in and what was happening when I could, I started to look at players who had only played on the offensive end because I felt I could teach them defense quicker than I could teach them how to shoot."

All of which is to say: while six-on-six remained in Iowa until 1993–94 and the skills and benefits often translated with the specialties of the six-on-six game, especially leading to some of the habits that created stars, the games were different enough that some assembly was required. It was no different for little Lisa Geske, who'd learned the five-on-five game in early childhood in Wisconsin before moving to Iowa, getting called for traveling in physical education class the year she arrived, not knowing she could only take two dribbles and had to stay on one side of the court. (Later on, Geske, who became Lisa Bluder, would master these rules pretty well.)

As the opportunities in women's basketball became more and more apparent, larger schools decided to start investing more heavily in their programs. Those who had arrived first weren't necessarily destined to stay on top. Cathy Rush had coached Stanley at Immaculata to three national titles and also coached the USA Basketball women's senior team. But by 1978 she'd left Immaculata and said this of her former program on a WBL broadcast where she was serving as color commentator: "Immaculata was a small college," she said during a timeout. "We only had 450 girls in school, and we completely dominated women's basketball at the time. Many of the girls that are playing now [in the WBL] are not from the UCLAs, the Iowa States. They're from very small schools…and pretty soon, I think we're going to see the players from UCLA, from Maryland, entering the league because that's where the good players are going right now. It's unfortunate for an Immaculata, it's unfortunate for the Delta States, but I think our era is over."

UCLA gave a full ride to Ann Meyers. The arms race was on, and even though Birdsong led the Hawkeyes to a winning record in 1978–79, it would prove to be her last season at the helm. She just didn't see Grant changing her mind and went back to school for business, though she and Grant would remain incredibly close friends for the next four decades. One of her players, Sue Beckwith, eventually endowed the head coaching position at Iowa. The title of P. Sue Beckwith, MD, Head Women's Basketball Coach was created in 2021 thanks to her donation and held first by Bluder, now by Jan Jensen.

Meanwhile, one of the small schools who dominated the AIAW years, Cheyney State, was finding success under the direction of Stringer, who'd risen to the job directing the school's basketball program for two primary reasons: she was willing to work for free, and when the athletic director asked all the Cheyney State teachers who would volunteer, no one else raised a hand.

But Stringer never minded an uphill battle. She sued her high school successfully for the right to join the cheerleading team—there hadn't been a Black cheerleader in a decade—and a judge agreed with her that racial discrimination was the reason why. She played four sports at Slippery Rock College, where she met her husband, Bill. And then as she pondered what to do with her life with her playing career over, coaching called to her.

No one else raised their hand. She was 23 years old. Over the next 11 years, she won 251 games at the helm of Cheyney State, fighting against that tide Rush mentioned and playing up—a Division II school playing a Division I schedule—and reached four straight AIAW tournaments, including the national title game in 1981–82 and the Sweet 16 in 1982–83. But that would prove to be Stringer's last year on campus. "I knew that we didn't have the money at Cheyney State," said Stringer as we sat and chatted in her New Jersey home in August 2024. "We didn't have the money, but we had the talent. We worked hard, and the players did some incredible things."

In the immediate aftermath of reaching the Final Four in 1982—as in right after the final buzzer—Stringer recalled her athletic director at Cheyney complaining to her that the school didn't have the money to send the team to the Final Four and had to rely on donations to get there. At Cheyney State budgets were tight as a matter of money, not a matter of choice. But at Iowa the thinking of Grant had changed as she watched other larger schools begin to grow their women's basketball programs, turning them into moneymakers, which in turn could fund other sports as well. "And at that point, I didn't see that Christine was going to change," Birdsong said about when she left following the 1978–79 season. Her successor, Judy McMullen, faced a similar internal landscape. "She only changed after she saw all these other universities getting ahead of her. Then she said, 'I need to focus on basketball.' That was when she was recruiting Vivian."

Stringer had received no shortage of job offers, usu-ally from high-major schools she'd managed to beat, in the decade-plus she led Cheyney State to improbable glory. But Iowa went to another level. Waiting for Vivian and Bill at the airport weren't high rollers or college boosters but a team of doctors to work with their daughter, Nina, who'd been stricken with spinal meningitis. Bill was given a job just down the hall from Vivian. But Vivian also knew one critical element to winning in Iowa and asked Grant point-blank. "I wanted to know: would I be able to recruit whoever, whoever it is that I wanted?" she said. "And she said, 'You can go all over the country and recruit.' So that's not a problem."

Grant also gave her a piece of advice, one seconded by Pat Summitt: go meet E. Wayne Cooley. And with that

Stringer was invited to the Iowa state tournament and experienced the revelation of Iowa girls basketball. "I heard about this place that packed the arena for girls basketball or women's basketball and I thought: *This is a strange thing.*" She saw men wearing tuxedos, the floor diligently being swept before each game, the passion of the place being displayed, and knew she could build the same thing at Carver-Hawkeye Arena.

She just talked it into reality—going everywhere she was invited to speak all over the state, spreading the word that the new epicenter of women's basketball in Iowa wasn't Des Moines but Iowa City. "Yes, I'm a Pisces. I dream," she told reporters at her introductory presser in April 1983. "And I work very hard to make my dreams become realities."

She knew that had to start at home with the recruiting of Lisa Becker, a 6'4" Iowa high school star who had been contacted by 225 schools—at a time when there weren't many more schools than that even recruiting for women's basketball. Stringer has never shied away from speaking her mind, so she didn't bother setting expectations on this score. She called the recruiting of Becker "an important first step in the establishment of this program."

She got Becker, and it set off shockwaves around the state. It was assumed if she stayed in state, she'd attend the prominent basketball power in Iowa: Drake. "Getting Lisa

Becker was like the first Iowa name to come out because they were all going to Drake really, but I think it was the first big Iowa name that went there," Bluder recalled in July 2024. "I don't know if that's what turned it around because Vivian recruited so heavily from the East Coast that getting Lisa Becker didn't help her get anybody from the East Coast unless you say, 'Well, here's the 6'5" center. Oh, [she'll be] fun to play with, have as a teammate.' But otherwise I think it helped her establish with the Iowa fan more so than recruiting."

For her part Stringer wasn't concerned about the transition from six-on-six to five-on-five, and neither was Becker, telling the *Quad City Times* just ahead of her freshman year, "It doesn't take as long for a player to make the transition as people think."

The very first game for Stringer's Iowa came against nationally ranked Drake. And while Drake won, it was by the slimmest of margins—58–56—in front of 3,165 people, representing the largest crowd for a women's sporting event in University of Iowa history at the time. The previous high for the women's basketball team had been 635, and Grant said her staff had laughed when she told them to prepare for 3,000 people at the opener. Becker, on her way to a legendary career at Iowa, finished with 14 points and nine rebounds. She won Big Ten Freshman of the Year honors. It didn't take very long at all to make the transition. Incidentally, the basketball genes roll deep in Becker's family—her sister, now Robin Pingeton, was also a star in Iowa six-on-six and now coaches women's basketball at Missouri, while Lisa's son, Michael Porter Jr., is a star wing for the NBA's Denver Nuggets.

The Lisas—Becker and Lisa Long, a Stringer recruit from New Jersey—turned the 7–20 record from the season before Stringer arrived into a 17–10 mark in her first season. A year after that, she added Michelle Edwards, who eventually played in the WNBA, and won 20 games. What did Stringer do to sell Edwards on Iowa? "She made the blueprint for what it takes," Edwards told me. "But it's often because it just doesn't encompass basketball. It encompasses the total person, and she really, she really allows players to become the best version of themselves while pushing them and loving them at the same time."

That season Stringer and the Lisas didn't sneak up on anyone, earning preseason rankings in both *Street & Smith's* and *Women's Court* magazines. One member of the media showed up for Iowa women's basketball the year before Stringer arrived. More than 30 were present to begin the 1984–85 season, a year Stringer told them she "hoped would live up to expectations."

She didn't have to worry. The Hawkeyes would go on to win 20 games for the first time in program history, finishing 14–4 in the Big Ten, and Stringer also saw her vision realized on February 3, 1985.

Just over a week before that game, Stringer published an open letter in ads, which ran in newspapers across the state. It read in part: "On Sunday, February 3 (1:00 PM) we play Big Ten champion and conference leader Ohio State. If we could defeat them, it would give us a very real chance to challenge for the Big Ten championship. I have another dream. It's to break the NCAA single-game attendance record…. I believe we can do it…. When we come out of that tunnel Sunday, I hope it's a day we'll all remember."

The previous women's attendance record was 10,622 when Kentucky hosted Old Dominion. Iowa drew 22,157. It drew that total because—even after pushing past Carver-Hawkeye Arena's official capacity of 15,000—fans poured into the stairways, drawing an official rebuke from the Iowa City fire marshal, and officials still had to turn 2,000 people away. Grant kept that rebuke framed in her office until the day she retired. "It brought tears to my eyes," Stringer said that day. "It is only appropriate that it happen here. Nowhere else could it have happened."

Even the opposing coach, a young upstart named Tara VanDerveer, expressed her appreciation for the crowd. "I'm a Buckeye all the way, but these Hawkeye fans—they did it! It's great to be a part of history."

Almost as an afterthought that day, Ohio State won 56–47. But the crowd opened everyone's eyes to what was happening in Iowa. "It was one of the key reasons why I wanted to go to the University of Iowa," said Jolette Law, who became the first great point guard for Stringer at Iowa, in a September 2024 interview. "The fan support and the way that they loved and they dove into basketball, women's basketball…. *Wow, I can play in front of screaming fans, loyal fans, night in and night out.* So as a young kid, 17, 18 years old, deciding on your university, their fan support was one of my key components that I took in consideration."

Stringer also drew the notice of a young Iowa coach, Geske, who'd grown up playing the six-on-six game at Linn-Mar High School in Marion, first finding the game when her father, Larry, built a hoop in the back of the house for her older brothers, Wayne and Scott. Neither one showed much interest in it. But she wore it out. "I'm the one that made the grass turn brown and made him have to trim the bushes a little bit more so I could shoot from farther out and that sort of thing," Lisa Geske Bluder said in a July 2024 interview. "I really am so glad that my dad put that hoop up."

Bluder was coached in high school by Sue Kudrna, now Nash, who'd made all-state second team in basketball—one of several sports she played—as a senior for Center Point High School. Like Lisa's dad, Sue's dad had also built a basketball hoop for her older brothers.

"My brothers weren't so much into basketball, but my sister that's a year-and-a-half older than I am, we played a lot of one-on-one together," Sue said in a July 2024 Zoom interview. "She was actually the post on our Center Point team, and I was the one that fed her a lot."

Then it was on to college, playing for Spencer first at Parsons, then in the mid-1970s on to William Penn, the early collegiate powerhouse run by the coach who also discovered Molly Van Benthuysen. "We loved playing Iowa back then," Nash remembered. Her Parsons team destroyed Iowa 73–22, "because the small colleges were getting all the good players back then."

And then? Even in this male-dominated field, Sue knew she wanted to coach. And so when Linn-Mar head coach Larry Schroeder offered her the chance out of college to be his top assistant and in charge of the offense, she leapt at it. The freshman sponge at Linn-Mar, Geske, saw that it was possible for a woman to advance in this field of coaching—as rare as it was back then. Sue saw something in Lisa that not many people did as a player. "Lisa was such a hard worker that she would stay after practice," Sue said. "And if we had late practice that night, we'd be there for another hour. I couldn't get her out of the gym. She was a gym rat, right? And people are saying, 'Why are you spending that much time with that girl? She's just not going to make it.' Well, by the time she was a senior in high school, she was one of the best in the metro…. I wanted so much to go back to those coaches and say, 'See, you know what? If you spend a little time with those kids that really want to give it their all, they'll become what you want them to become.'"

Despite all her hard work, just as with Molly, Lisa never quite made it to the state tournament as a player. "It's still bad memories," said Bluder with a rueful laugh. "It really is. I wanted to play at state so badly. I went every year to the girls state tournament. It was a big deal here—packed. It was pomp and circumstance. There were only 16 teams from the whole state that went. There weren't any divisions back then. It was just a whole week of celebrating really the female basketball player, and I wanted to be a part of that so badly. So, yeah, it's still, it's still bitter."

From there it was on to Northern Iowa for Lisa, who had sprouted to 5'10½" by her sophomore year in high school and earned a half-scholarship to Northern Iowa—a notion made possible by Sue's path. "And that's the first time I really thought, *Hey, you can do this in college,*" Lisa said. "I never really even thought about that." Iowa didn't even contact her for recruiting purposes. But Northern Iowa wanted her after an open tryout—the first time in years she'd played five-on-five ball again.

But at Northern Iowa, she found herself playing in front of 200, 300 people. Her teammates from other states were astounded that she'd grown up watching girls basketball on television. Her primary focus in college was to major in accounting, not prepare for a life of basketball coaching. "I went to my first accounting class," she said, "and we covered all of my high school accounting in about two weeks, and the accountant was in the library all the time. And I thought, *This is not what I want to do.* I wanted to play basketball."

She took a job doing some graphic design—that had been her minor at UNI—but she stayed involved in the game any chance she could. When Stringer's Iowa team came to play at UNI, she announced the game. She'd officiate games whenever she could. But when her boyfriend, David, proposed to her, she reached out to the local schools in Davenport, where he lived and worked, and none of them even replied to her with a rejection letter. She and Dave met when she was still in high school. An athlete himself, Dave immediately began coming to all of her games. "He just understood how important sports was to me," she recalled.

Finally, just before the 1984–85 school year started, Dave's across-the-street neighbor pointed out that the local college, St. Ambrose, had an ad in the paper for a women's basketball coach. Lisa returned home from the interview and took David to lunch. "I said Dave, 'I've got good news and bad news,'" Lisa remembered. "'The good news is I got the job. The bad news is it pays $2,400 a year.'"

But Dave did not hesitate, telling Lisa she had to take the job. And with her negotiating skills, Lisa even got them all the way up to a starting salary of $2,500. "I was given an office at the very end of the hall that I shared with the men's basketball assistant," Lisa said. "And it was tiny. It was not more than probably seven feet wide and a little bit deeper.... I don't even have a telephone in there, so if I need to use the telephone I go to the secretary's desk for the athletic department to use the telephone. That was a big deal. And after a while, the men's assistant moved out, and the volleyball head coach moved in."

She drove her eight players in a red van to Clark College and won her opener. It became a habit. Her St. Ambrose teams were good immediately, going 18–13 in her first season at the helm and 29–3 by Year Three, when they reached the NAIA postseason. In her final two years at St. Ambrose, the team went a combined 70–3 with two NAIA Fab Four appearances to show for it. And her summers were spent reading everything she could get her hands on about coaching, attending every clinic she could find, and coaching at the girls basketball camps under, yes, Stringer. She even convinced one of Stringer's players to give her tapes of Stringer's practices just so she could learn from her, but her plans were foiled because, as Bluder put it, "Vivian was a low talker."

But this was her calling. She knew that, even though her parents didn't fully understand it was a profession until she was a candidate for a head coaching job at Northern Iowa. "I was so excited," Lisa remembered. "I mean, I loved it. Instant love, right? You go to practice and you're in charge of a practice and you're leading these young women now, who are only like three years younger than me, two years younger some of them, I mean, so that's pretty strange. But at the same time, I fell in love with it instantly and just wanted to do it. Then I wanted to do it forever. That clicked in like, *This is awesome*."

Dave was all in, too. St. Ambrose bumped her up to $11,000 a year, and Lisa Bluder was on her way.

Stringer's Iowa program needed Lisa Becker. Bluder's St. Ambrose rose to Fab Four level with her sister, Robin Becker. But the bigger schools were asserting themselves more and more. She'd turned down her alma mater the year before, but when Drake came calling, the 29-year-old Bluder took the opportunity to take the helm of the storied school. She only found out about the job because at the awards ceremony for her to receive NAIA Coach of the Year she happened to be sitting right behind a woman on the Drake coaching search committee who urged her to apply. She did and got the job. It came as a relief, according to Jensen, a junior on that Drake team. "The uncertainty is over. That's good," Jensen said to Jane Burns of *The Des Moines Register*. "There's direction again; there's someone to share the excitement of the future with."

Has there been a more prophetic quote in a story of a new coach's hiring? Bluder's formula was simple—as she laid it out that day—and instantly recognizable. "We'll fast break at every opportunity," she said. "We need to get back on track and get the Iowans back at Drake."

Jensen was such an Iowan. The legend from Kimballton scored 66 points per game in her senior season, leading Elkhorn-Kimballton to the state tournament. She scored 105 points in a single game against Villisca on February 19, 1987. She'd picked Drake over Creighton, Kansas, Missouri, Northwestern, and Harvard. Iowa had been in on her early, and she said, "You could see Vivian was coming, but Drake had the tradition."

It helped that her grandmother, Dorcas Andersen, had played on that very same floor.

Andersen told *The Des Moines Register* in March 1987: "Enough already about me, I'm just a shadow. Jan and her teammates are in the spotlight now." Andersen was inducted into the Iowa Girls High School Athletic Union Hall of Fame in 1970; Jensen joined her in 1993.

Playing Bluder's style, Jensen averaged 29.6 points per game in her senior year at Drake. She went overseas to play for a year in Germany—Bluder insists that she'd have been a WNBA player easily if the league had been around when Jensen graduated, to which Jensen replied, "It's nice to hear your old coach still believes in you"—before returning home. She was adrift despite her excellent academic record.

But Bluder hired her as a grad assistant, and then when one of her full-time assistants left, she added Jensen as a full-time assistant. "And 30 years later, here I am," Jensen said.

Jensen's teammate at Drake, Jenni Fitzgerald, the point guard to Jensen's post, joined the Drake staff with Jensen in 1991. She stayed with Jensen and Bluder through the end of the 2023–24 season, too.

Jensen had considered herself straight throughout high school and college and was even engaged to be married to a man. But she realized something. "Maybe this wasn't tracking," she said. "And it was time for some soul-searching." Jensen called off the engagement and spoke at length to her friend and former teammate at Drake, Julie Fitzpatrick, who had come out a few years earlier. "I was figuring out my life, and Julie had figured out her life, but we'd always been really good friends," Jensen said in an August 2024 interview. "Julie was the epitome of awesomeness, and if you ask any of the Drake circle—she was team captain, highly successful, just unbelievable level of integrity, and all the things. So we were friends, but she had come out a little bit earlier. So we're fortunate in the sense we had that friendship before, and I had someone as that confidante, and then we ended up together."

In Jensen's mind that left two key questions. What would her hometown reaction be? "I just wanted to continue," Jensen said. "I grew up in the greatest place, the greatest era. I just didn't want to lose it, and I didn't need them to sign a paper that says, 'Oh, I love you, and I totally switched my thinking about gay relationships,' right?.... [That] wasn't how I needed to do it. And not one person in my home, not one to this day, not one person ever disowned me. And so when I come home, everybody's great."

The other, more pressing question: what would she do for a living since she knew she didn't want to be a burden on Bluder's staff, and negative recruiting against LGBTQ coaches was rampant at that time. So she entered Bluder's office to offer her resignation. "I never wanted to be a hindrance to anybody else's success," Jensen said. "If I was by myself and I'm starting up a business, well, then it's on me, right? Because if people don't want to do business with me, then I've got to keep figuring it out. But if you're part of an organization of which you could negatively impact their success, that's what was hard for me." But for Bluder it wasn't even a question. Ultimately, Jensen became Bluder's ace in the hole for recruiting for three decades.

By 1993 Stringer's Iowa team reached the Final Four. Just one Iowa native, Molly Tideback, logged minutes for the team. It was a triumph, but the year contained more pain than anyone should have to bear—most notably, when Vivian's husband, Bill, died of a heart attack on Thanksgiving Day.

Jensen, meanwhile, was inducted into the Iowa Girls High School Athletic Union Hall of Fame. Grandmother Dorcas traveled with her to Des Moines to see her receive the honor. "I'm kind of floating some of the time to think, *Here I am, 90 years old, and I'm fortunate*," Andersen told *The Des Moines Register*. "I always had an inkling that if anybody would make the Hall of Fame, why, it would certainly be her."

Jensen, Bluder, and Fitzgerald's Drake team posted a 15–13 winning record that season. By 1994–95 they had Drake in the NCAA Tournament. It would become a habit—even as University of Iowa's program slipped in the latter half of the 1990s. The reason was simple. Stringer had moved onto Rutgers. It was not an easy decision for her at all. She told me point-blank if Bill hadn't died, she thinks she'd still be coaching on the Iowa sidelines to this day. But every time she looked over at the seat in the first row he'd occupied—now empty—she was overcome with emotions she wouldn't let her team see. "It was a good life," Stringer said. Her sisters moved to Iowa and still live there. She remembered complaining to them before they joined her in Iowa: "I spend so much money because at the time that's when AT&T was charging by the minute. They gouged the heck out of us."

But while tragedy altered Stringer's track away from Iowa—she was joined in Piscataway, New Jersey, by her old point guard, Law, who retired from playing with the Harlem Globetrotters so she could "pour into" the coach who had done so much for her—it was a near-tragedy that sent a Bluder on course for Iowa City. In the summer of 1997, Dave was hit by a car and left in a coma for three days. When he came to, he was unable to put together a three-piece puzzle. Meanwhile, Lisa was pregnant with her first child. "I'm thinking, *Well, that's the end of life as I know it*," she remembered. "So that's when I think my career is probably over. But then we went through that summer, again, my staff and Jenni really probably held things together a lot for me during that time, and I had Hannah that summer."

After Dave went back to work for a spell, he and Lisa had a real-talk conversation about how the next facet of their life should look. "He goes, 'I feel like your career has more trajectory than mine,'" Lisa recalled her husband, who was the vice president of a bank, saying. "'I feel like I can get back into my career easier than if you would quit to try to get back into your career,' which is true. And so he came up with the idea to stay home with Hannah. And then along came Emma and David, too. So he quit his job in '98 and has not worked since outside the home full time. So that was huge. And I'm going back to the question you asked.... Did I think I could do both? Yeah, the only reason was because of David—the only reason."

The devout husband was right about her trajectory. Lisa and Drake were getting more than their share of Iowa kids, while Stringer's successor, Angie Lee, struggled to replicate the success her former coach had enjoyed. Bluder had actually been a finalist for the Iowa job before Lee got it. When the Hawkeyes let Lee go, Grant turned her attention toward finding the leader of the program, and Bluder, Jensen, and Fitzgerald were all coming off of another successful season at Drake. Since the Bulldogs played in the competitive mid-major Missouri Valley Conference, that meant entering the NCAA Tournament with just a No. 8 seed. There was a collective understanding that just as Stringer had maxed out Cheyney State, the trio had done the same at Drake.

Bluder had a phone interview with Grant but felt like she didn't sell herself enough and called Grant to tell her so. Grant agreed, and they had a second interview, which went much better, according to Bluder. "I really wanted that job," she said. "It was 40 minutes from my parents, where I grew up. It was in the Big Ten. And I knew the possibilities that could happen there at Iowa because I'd seen it happen with Coach Stringer."

That left Jensen with a choice, too. As a leading assistant for Bluder and an accomplished Drake alum in her own right, the Drake head coaching job was hers for the taking. But Jensen felt her place was with Bluder. Ditto for Fitzgerald, who moved to Iowa with them. The team that built the Caitlin Clark era was thus preserved—two years before Clark's birth. "It was three components," Jensen said. "No. 1, that loyalty. No. 2, I'd grown up at Drake and I loved it. And so a lot of times you're...just leaving your comfort zone. You've got to leave it. But in some ways, I was leaving the comfort zone. Leave because staying the head coach would have been uncomfortable, but leaving and going to Iowa was definitely a comfort zone." Still, she had doubts in her mind: "Did I want to be a gay head coach at that time?" And three was the tantalizing possibility. They'd lost several recruits that year to "so-called Power Five teams." As Jensen put it, "The winds were changing, and maybe we could do this thing over there, and then that became the driving force."

That coaching triumvirate won right away and never stopped winning. With Lee's players they won 21 games and a Big Ten Tournament to boot. They reached the NCAA Tournament seven times by 2010, captured a Big Ten regular-season crown in 2007–08 with five players from Iowa. In 2005 they welcomed back Stringer, who, of course, went to Rutgers and kept on winning. Imagine a more resounding affirmation for a coach's abilities than to take three different programs to the Final Four and have those three programs be Cheyney State in 1982, Iowa in 1993, and Rutgers in 2000. (She made it with Rutgers again in 2007 for good measure.)

Law was with her when Rutgers came to play in the Hawkeye Challenge in 2005. "When we walked into that arena, I told her, 'I know you're looking over there,'" Law said, referring to Bill's old seat. "But when we walked in that arena, I was just like, *Oh my god, I got chills. This is home.* But it was weird, sitting on the opposite side. Normally, we aren't on this side…. But I was just trying to be there in her ear, 'We're back here now. God brought us back here for a reason.'" Stringer won 57–51 before 3,620 fans. Those crowd numbers had become par for the course at Carver-Hawkeye, but it was larger than the one for her first game way back in 1983, which had set the record by a factor of five.

Bluder, Jensen, and Iowa kept on winning. They made every NCAA Tournament but two in the 2010s, reaching the Elite Eight in 2018–19. Still, a Final Four had eluded them. During this run, at a seventh-grade AAU game in Chicago, Bluder watched when a young guard took the floor and captivated her right away. "[I] heard about her from Jan. Okay, first time I've seen her was at that point," Bluder said. Was it immediately apparent this was a player on a different level? "Yeah, yeah," said Bluder, laughing. "The recognition was immediate. It's the way she carried herself, her ball handling skills, passing skills, and basically her moxie, and really she was physically mature back then… she's scrawny now, but back then she wasn't little like some seventh graders you think of being little. She wasn't little back then."

Jensen remembers the first few plays of her Caitlin Clark experience from that time. "Between the legs, step-back three fade," said Jensen, who could see it clearly in her mind as she was telling me. "Next trip down dribbled it right before half court, threw it on a dime in stride to a kid who blew the layup."

By the fall of 2016, Clark showed up as a freshman at Dowling Catholic. "Caitlin Clark was as good as advertised,"

The Ankeny Register & Press Citizen wrote of her first game. "Maybe even better." She had 21 points on just eight shots along with three assists, the shape of the game as identifiable then as now.

Bluder and Jensen knew the stakes of getting Clark. She'd told Clark directly that after Iowa reached the Elite Eight and lost to Baylor in 2019. "I flew home the very next day. All my staff went to the Final Four from there, [but] I went home, Jan and I, so that we could go do a home visit with Caitlin," Bluder said. "And we went into her house and just said: 'Listen, we are one game away from the Final Four, one game. You come, we can do this.' And so we put that in her head."

Clark first chose Notre Dame, her parents' preferred choice. She told Bluder that on the phone, ruining a beautiful day on the Iowa campus, where Bluder was watching Hawkeyes field hockey at Christine Grant Field. But for three weeks, the official announcement never came.

"And then her AAU assistant coach called me and said, 'I think Caitlin's having some second thoughts. Would you still have room?'" Bluder said.

Spoiler alert: she still had room for her at Iowa.

That night, Lisa and Dave were eating at Orchard Green, a restaurant in Iowa City, and sitting down by the fireplace. The phone rang. It was Clark. "I go outside to take the phone call right out to the parking lot, and she tells me that, 'Well, if I was changing, would you still want me?' And I'm like, 'Uh, yeah!' So then I went in, and we ordered a bottle of champagne and then we took one over to Jan's house. We celebrated with her. It was pretty awesome."

As they celebrated, Jensen felt as if she'd finally get to see her faith in Bluder fully realized. Though she called herself "a post-biased person," Jensen knew the value of a truly game-changing guard. "Lisa called me, and I was like, 'Oh my gosh.' And so she says, 'We're coming over.' And I just remember amazing elation and excitement because we just knew that she was going to be a catalyst," Jensen said. "And I had believed in Lisa so much that I'd always said, 'Man, if we could just get some of the key players that some of the other people got at times, I really wanted to see what we could do because I think Lisa is such a great mastermind of different things.' And that's what I was so excited about."

Everything had finally come together. Iowa girls basketball six-on-six, distilled into a five-on-five world. An Iowa girl with more talent than anyone could remember had grown up in the shadow of the state tournament, infused by generations of belief in the game, the thrills of it and the value of the work, the extra pass, and the good-to-great shot with more talent than anyone could remember. Finally, there was the infrastructure to maximize her success at the school, college, and the pros, and the ability for a worldwide audience to take in her greatness, to celebrate it, to reward it financially for Caitlin Clark to stand on the shoulders of Dorcas Andersen and the Van Horne Hornettes and Molly Bolin and Vivian Stringer and Jolette Law and Jan Jensen and Lisa Bluder and then on high ground prepare to elevate those who come after her as well.

That night at Jensen's house, could they see all that? Bluder said, laughing: "No crystal ball here!"

Or as Jensen put it: "I mean, you could see All-American, but can we see this?" Jensen said. "No. I said, 'Definitely she was going to be one of the best in the Big Ten,' right? But until you get there, and you saw that motor, then think, *Okay, now we got a shot.* You can see the All-Americans and All-Big Ten performers. They have that potential, and you've just got to put them in the right place, and they've got to respond to you. But did we see her becoming the face of the world? No."

Afterword

While it may have come as a shock to many when Lisa Bluder decided to step down as head coach at Iowa, it came—as so many of the decision points in her life did—from a conversation with Dave. "Even when I went to the draft, it still wasn't in my mind at that point," Lisa said. "It was emotional for me to see her go in the draft. I think that probably if Caitlin would have come back, I would have come back, right? But I do think that her leaving, it was just a great opportunity for me to leave. We have good kids coming in, but it was so many young kids, and I was tired. I was really tired after this season. I mean, because we had our foreign trip last year, too, so we practiced all of August, and it was two years straight…. And so Dave and I went off on vacation, and we started talking about [retirement] right away as soon as we got on vacation. And we like to hike, and so we're hiking in the mountains and Phoenix…and just keep having these conversations."

A chance to help Emma, her daughter, plan her wedding. A chance to watch David, her son, play his senior year at Grinnell while unencumbered by an iPad to break down film of Iowa. A chance to relax and enjoy her newfound fame—*oh, David Letterman wants to go watch the Fever? Jason Sudeikis wants to come to dinner? Sounds good!* "It's amazing," Bluder said. "I walk into games, and there's so many Iowa fans. I go into the game, I see Iowa jerseys. Now it's getting a little bit more Indiana 22, but it was definitely at the beginning all Iowa stuff. And it was just so cool to see that. And you're so proud of that, that these fans care so much about your team and your players that they're going out of their way to support them. I go see the Aces play the Fever, and I am flying out of Des Moines, and half or more of that plane is wearing Iowa stuff and is going to the game. It's unbelievable."

Bluder maintains that her legacy is entirely tied to Clark, though anyone who won 936 games—including 643 at Iowa—before Clark arrived built a pretty significant legacy a long time ago. "I was so happy that someone like Lisa Bluder got the recognition she did the last two years because that is who Lisa Bluder has been at Drake," Jan Jensen said. "That's who she was when she was at St. Ambrose. And she's pretty beloved by most every player that's ever played for her. And she's had a level of integrity that is one of the best. I don't think she has too many enemies. You might not have liked her because she won a lot.... What I love is I think she should be an incredible role model in how you succeed in a profession and you left it better than you found it. You moved the needle more than anybody has moved it or arguably as much.... I think the way she did it constantly and consistently, to get to stay at the place she wanted to be at for a quarter of a century and not get let go, not have any major issues, and then leave it on your own terms, that doesn't happen very often."

There was only one choice to take the helm at Iowa when Bluder retired, and it was Jensen. There would have been a revolt in the state of Iowa otherwise. Bluder won't push her ideas on Jensen—it's Jensen's program now, she said—but she's there if needed. Bluder has been nominated for the Naismith Basketball Hall of Fame. So has Molly Bolin. If there's any justice in the world, they'll both be elected.

C. Vivian Stringer has retired, too. She served the women's game for half a century. She's earned the rest, the adulation. There's typically a get-together at the Final Four of past players and assistants in her honor called the CVS Brunch. She didn't make it to the Final Four, so in August of 2024 they brought the festivities to her, gathering at her home in New Jersey. And she got to watch Betnijah Laney, the daughter of one of her Cheyney State players, Yolanda Laney, win a WNBA title with the New York Liberty. Stringer coached Betnijah, too.

She'd had a chance to leave women's basketball 25 years ago now. John Thompson Jr., the venerated Georgetown men's basketball head coach, was preparing to retire in 1999, and Georgetown was letting him name his successor. He wanted his successor to be Stringer. But Stringer remembered a promise she'd made years ago to Tara VanDerveer. On one USA Basketball trip, the two coaches who'd once stood and marveled at the 22,857 people gathered in Carver-Hawkeye Arena just because Stringer had asked them to come came to an agreement. "She and I talked about the fact that we shouldn't ever step outside and coach men," Stringer said. "Don't coach the men because we needed to give our services to women. And that's what I thought of when he asked me."

Stringer turned him down. And though she wouldn't take credit for all that had happened on her watch—if there is an Iowa characteristic more significant than shooting or passing, it might be an unwillingness to take credit for seismic changes, and that's true for both the Iowa natives and adopted daughters like Stringer—she did think the meeting of Bluder and Clark was the perfect alchemy of people, place, and time. "It was only appropriate that the notoriety that she gathered was something very special and she could handle, she did handle all of that in a very positive way," Stringer said. "I don't know that there's another who could have."

Acknowledgments

Since the very start of Caitlin Clark's collegiate career at Iowa, I have been reporting on and processing her rise within the framework of the women's basketball world. I have the privilege of covering every single day at The Next Women's Basketball Newsroom (www.thenexthoops.com) and The IX Women's Sports Newsletter (www.theixsports.com).

Making sure I could properly document not only her rise but why and how it happened required the help of so many people who not only created this moment but allowed me to hear their incredible stories and memories from that build.

I am particularly grateful for the time I received from Lisa Bluder, David Bluder, Molly Kazmer, Sue Kudrna Nash, Larry Wiebke, Evelyn Brehm, Lin Dunn, Jolette Law, Jim Schnack, and Lark Birdsong. Thank you to all of you for helping me reconstruct the past and contextualize the present. And every single one of you is owed a debt of gratitude from women's basketball.

I must single out two people even amid this group who spent hours with me: Jan Jensen, who shared both her own experience and her grandmother's journals with me so we could attach the past to the present together, and C. Vivian

Stringer, who so graciously invited me into her home and shared her unparalleled wisdom and insights into a women's basketball landscape she's done as much as anyone to create and bloom. One of the great joys of this work is spending time with people who have accomplished things, often underappreciated, that have changed countless lives.

And a huge thank you to Caitlin, Kate Martin, Christie Sides, Kelsey Mitchell, Lexie Hull, and many other players, coaches, and executives in the WNBA, both named and unnamed in here, who found time to give me insight and context within the whirlwind that was the 2024 WNBA season.

Thank you to Liz Galloway-McQuitter and the incredible trailblazers of the WBL for introducing me to Molly and working day and night to share their stories with a public who still does not fully realize: without the WBL, there is no WNBA.

Thank you to Triumph Books for realizing the importance of telling these stories within women's sports. I am indebted to the vision of my editors, Jeff Fedotin and Jesse Jordan; the vital support of Clarissa Young, Stefani Szenda, and Bill Ames; and, of course, to Noah Amstadter for fostering this space.

Thank you to Jane Burns, an incredible journalist who covered so much of this history herself and offers an enthusiastic guided tour to all things Iowa basketball and might be the only person in America who loves cheese even more than I do.

Thank you to a century of journalists in and around Iowa who helped create a first draft of the history of this incredible sport.

I could not imagine my work life without The Next and The IX family, especially Jenn Hatfield, Kathleen Gier, and Alex Simon, who made it possible for me to finish this book.

I can't imagine better or more enthusiastic supporters than my in-laws, Hilary and Jason Schwartz, who never stopped rooting me on even as the two of them fought Jason's cancer diagnosis so bravely. All of us who knew him will miss Jason more than I can possibly say.

And to my parents, Myrna and Ira, you have always encouraged me to find my own path and tell the stories that matter to me. You never miss a chance to make things easier or happier for our immediate family. I do not take for granted that we get to see each other when this happens or how much you care about me and everyone in Chome 2.

To Mirabelle and Juliet: what girls and women in Iowa fought for over the past century is simple: a pathway to discovering the maximum joy and achievement out of life possible not from artificial limitations but rather from talent and skill alone. That you have so enthusiastically joined this fight leaves me more optimistic about a world that sorely needs you.

To Rachel: everything else is secondary to us and the life we keep building together.

To every girl who ever played basketball in Iowa: I hope this book serves as a monument to your joys, your sorrows, your triumphs on and off the court, and most of all, what you made possible. Because you did this.

Sources

Personal Interviews

Caitlin Clark

Lin Dunn

Cathy Engelbert

Lisa Bluder

David Bluder

Jan Jensen

Lark Birdsong

Molly Kazmer

Larry Wiebke

Evelyn Brehm

Sue Kudrna Nash

Jim Schnack

Jolette Law

Jane Burns

Michelle Edwards

C. Vivian Stringer

Kate Martin

Monika Czinano

Gabbie Marshall

McKenna Warnock

Lexie Hull

Kelsey Mitchell

Aliyah Boston

Christie Sides

Stephanie White

Websites

AcrossTheTimeline.com

Basketball-reference.com

Census.gov

DMCPC.org

ESPNPressRoom.com

Forbes.com

HawkeyeRecap.com

History.com

IHSA.org

IowaDataCenter.org

Mason City Globe-Gazette

Maxpreps.com

NCAA.org

Offenburger.com

ScottyMoore.net

SportsBusinessJournal.com

SportsMediaWatch.com

TheNextHoops.com

Periodicals

Atlantic News Telegraph

The (Clarksville, Tennessee*) Leaf-Chronicle*

Connecticut Post

The Des Moines Register

Iowa City Press-Citizen

The (Iowa Falls) *Hardin County Times*

The Moravia Union

The New York Times

Sioux City Journal

Smithsonian magazine

Time magazine

Books

From Six-On-Six to Full Court Press: *A Century of Iowa Girls'*
Basketball, Janice A. Beran

The Only Dance in Iowa: A History of Six-Player Girls' Basket-
ball, David (Max) McIlwain

Misc.

LPGA Media

NCAA External Equity Review, Kaplan, Hecker & Fink,
August, 2021

Sport, Business and Management: An International Journal,
September 2021

WQAD News 8